THE
MAKING OF AMERICA
SERIES

BEAVER FALLS
GEM OF BEAVER COUNTY

STANDING ON THE BEAVER FALLS/NEW BRIGHTON BRIDGE. Looking up the Beaver River, you can see the 10th Street Bridge and one of the many falls on the Beaver River. (Photographer, Paul Couderc.)

THE
MAKING OF AMERICA
SERIES

BEAVER FALLS
GEM OF BEAVER COUNTY

KENNETH BRITTEN

ARCADIA

Published by Arcadia Publishing,
an imprint of Tempus Publishing, Inc.
2 Cumberland Street
Charleston, SC 29401

Printed in Great Britain.

Library of Congress Catalog Card Number: 2002104050

For all general information contact Arcadia Publishing at:
Telephone 843-853-2070
Fax 843-853-0044
E-Mail sales@arcadiapublishing.com

For customer service and orders:
Toll-Free 1-888-313-2665

Visit us on the Internet at http://www.arcadiapublishing.com

FRONT COVER: *VIEW OF LOWER BEAVER FALLS COVERED BRIDGE, C. 1890. This is the first of several bridges that would be built between Beaver Falls and New Brighton.*

CONTENTS

ACKNOWLEDGMENTS

The author is indebted to his fellow members of the Beaver Falls Historical Society and to the staff of the Carnegie Free Library of Beaver Falls for their support, encouragement, and help. A special thanks to Ginny Brandon for typing the manuscript so it could be sent to the publisher. Also a special thank you to Bertha Greco, the hostess and docent of the museum, for her patience and understanding when I rifled through the society's collection of photos and manuscripts looking for material. Special recognition is due Sue Martella of Suzy's Photo for her ability to coax latent images from faded photographs for us. Untold chapters of local history have emerged from the holdings of the Beaver Falls Museum and the Beaver County Historical Research Center located in the Carnegie Free Library.

This book is dedicated to the following individuals for their contributions to Beaver Falls, without which it would not be the great city it is today: Gladys Fair Frumen Hum, J. Neal Mathews, James Reynolds Jr. (our late mayor), the Lytle sisters (Ethel and Agnes), Miss Patricia Covert (a great history teacher), Wilda Roberts and Ferndetta Caldwell, Sidney Kane, Laree Riley (another teacher of history), Alice Sterrett, Mr. and Mrs. Edward Shali Sr., Mr. Eugene Jannuzi and wife Margaret, also Eugene Tronzo for his artwork contribution, Myer Berkman and members of the Jewish Community, Reverend Calvin Brown and members of the African-American Community, and last but not least the sisters from Mt. Gallitzin, Seaton Hall, and Divine Providence.

Speaking for generations past and those yet to come, the author wishes to express profound appreciation to those who provide the steady flow of archival material for the collection at the Beaver Falls Historical Society Museum. Their contributions are valued beyond measure and allow us to celebrate our past as a reaffirmation of our faith in the future.

All this would count for little if not for the many people who find their appreciation for the present enhanced by an intimate knowledge of the past. To all who have contributed to this effort of sharing the elements of growth and greatness of this magnificent community, the author extends his deepest appreciation.

INTRODUCTION

Beaver Falls, known as Brighton before its incorporation, is located in the western corner of Pennsylvania. During its first 150 years, residents of the town built it into a self-supporting community committed to family values. Extensive industrial development occurred during this period and the city was described as "one of the most well-established manufacturing towns in Western Pennsylvania."

In 1945, several residents formed the Beaver Falls Historical Society. Fifty-five years later, another group of Beaver Falls residents came together in the same spirit of preservation to compile an unprecedented pictorial history that chronicled the unique story of Beaver Falls and its people. Released in time for the 200th anniversary celebrations of Beaver County, *Beaver Falls* was a fitting tribute to a cherished community. With the success of that book, the historical society received many requests for a more detailed history of the city. A detailed history was published in 1969, but it has long since been out of print. We hope that this current book, *Beaver Falls: Gem of Beaver County*, fulfills that need.

1. Birth of a Town

Beaver County, Pennsylvania, being situated on one of the main routes from the Atlantic coast to the Mississippi Valley in the eighteenth century, was rich in Native American life and legend.

When the French and English first penetrated the wilderness of this area to explore its wonders in search of the valued beaver pelt or to carve out new homes for themselves, they encountered groups of natives living along the banks of a stream called Amockwi-Sipu or Amockwi-Hanne. This name, translated into English from the language of the Delaware, became Beaver Stream or Beaver River. The Delaware gave this name to the stream because it was a favorite home of the beaver. The Beaver River abounded with this prized animal.

The larger stream into which the Amockwi-Hanne flows was called O-he-yu, meaning Beautiful River. This name, given by the Senecas who lived at the headwaters near what is now the Pennsylvania–New York state line, was used by the Native Americans to indicate the entire river system. O-he-yu, through interpretation of sounds of the guttural Indian language rather than translation, became the Ohio.

Native Americans living in this area when the European settlers arrived were of the great Algonquin family. This was composed of tribes of Delaware and Shawnee along with the Iroquois or six nations, also known by their Indian name of Mengwi. From these so-called six nations came small bands of Iroquois warriors under the leadership of eminent chiefs, several of whom were located within the present boundaries of Beaver County.

Their particular chiefs managed the affairs of each village while general interests, national affairs, and a great council assembly composed of the chiefs of the tribes conducted the affairs of war and peace.

In 1770, a mission of the Moravians was established among the Algonquin Indians and the town known as Friendenstadt was built near the Delaware village called Kuskuskee. Many Native Americans were converted by the Moravians and it appears that for a time, the settlers and Indians enjoyed a more or less peaceful co-existence.

Two Delaware chiefs, Kelelamand (called Killbuck), and Koquethagchton (called White-Eyes) took up the hatchet on the side of the colonists, but were

PLATT MAP. This map shows original surveys of the area that would later be Beaver Falls. Notice the outline of the property owned by John White.

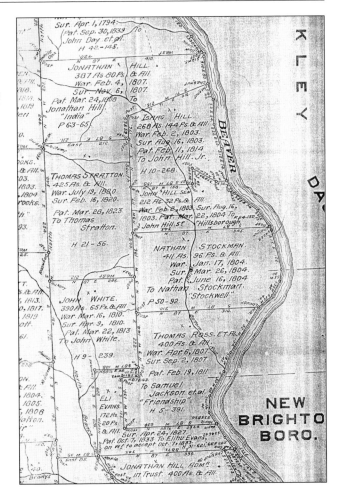

unable to control the young warriors of their nations and restrain them from joining the Shawnee and other hostile tribes.

In order that the frontiers would not be completely exposed, the colonists formed scouting parties to range the Ohio River from Beaver Creek downstream. Meanwhile, in the fall of 1778, militia under English brigadier general Lachlan McIntosh moved from Fort Pitt (Pittsburgh) down the Ohio to the mouth of Beaver Creek, where they built Fort McIntosh at Beaver.

Fort McIntosh became the scene of an important treaty in 1785 between the Pennsylvania commissioners Francis Johnston and Samuel J. Atlee and the chiefs of the Wyandots, Chippewa, Delaware, and Ottawa. The result of this treaty was the release of all prisoners taken by the Native Americans. It also resulted in the purchase of the territory that now includes the counties of Potter, Elk, Tioga, McKean, Warren, Crawford, Venango, Forest, Clarion, Jefferson, Cameron, Butler, Lawrence, and Mercer, along with parts of the counties of Beaver, Allegheny, Armstrong, Indiana, Clinton, Clearfield, Erie, and Bradford.

The Americans paid the various Indian tribes a total of $7,000, which was a small amount for such a large tract of land, unless one considers that these tribes fought as allies of the British in the Revolutionary War and were considered defeated enemies who could have been dispossessed without compensation.

Following the close of the war, several expeditions against the Native Americans quieted them and reduced the danger of their forays, and the occupation of Fort McIntosh became less important. In 1788, it was ordered demolished. Orders were also issued for construction of a blockhouse a few miles up the Beaver River at a small stream now known as Blockhouse Run in New Brighton.

The relationship between the settlers and the Native Americans for the next few years seemed mostly peaceful, with some incidents of murder and reprisal perpetrated by both sides. One such incident took place at the Blockhouse in 1791 when Samuel Brady, a former Army captain with a group of Virginia Raiders, attacked and killed four Indians (three men and one woman) while they were trading with one William Wilson. Charges and counter-charges followed. The Native Americans killed by Brady were alleged to have been in possession of articles known to have been the property of a family that had some time before been murdered at Mingo Bottom in Steubenville, Ohio.

Such incidents continued to build tensions until 1794 when General Wayne, with a newly trained army named "The Legion of the United States," moved

PENNSYLVANIA CANAL. This picture shows one of the canal locks on the Beaver River, which is on the New Brighton side.

down the Ohio and met about 2,000 Native Americans under Blue-Jacket, a chief of the Shawnee, and routed them in a decisive battle. This victory brought lasting peace to the western borders, removed the menace of Indian hostility, and opened the remaining land within the limits of Beaver County to settlement.

Some of the Native Americans known to the early settlers of this area who were influential to their way of life were a Delaware woman known as Queen Aliquippa, who lived for a time near the site of Aliquippa, the town named for her; Chief Logan, who lived at a Mingo Indian Village at the mouth of the Beaver opposite Shingas Town, known as Logans Town (Rochester); and Chief White-Eyes, who was a warm friend to the Moravian missionaries and who, although he never made a profession of religion himself, was known to have persuaded many other Indians to embrace it.

The record of the first whites who set foot in the valley of the Beaver carries the mind back to a time when no white man dared settle permanently in it, antedating the history of our country by about 28 years.

The first group of white men who were here, so far as history shows, was a party under Conrad Weiser in 1748 sent by the governor and council of Pennsylvania to ascertain the strength of the Native Americans in this area. The contest between the English and French for supremacy in these forest wilds had become desperately earnest and many plans were laid to counteract the influence of the French with the Indians. The English in eastern Pennsylvania sent out the expedition under Weiser, who was an Indian interpreter and a man of strong natural abilities and talents. With him was George Groghan, a trader among the Native Americans, who had a trading post the same year on the site of Beaver.

Weiser and party arrived at Logstown—a settlement situated on the Ohio River about 14 miles above the mouth of the Beaver River—on August 26, 1748. They made this settlement their headquarters. During their stay here, a few of the more adventurous of the party started, on August 29, to explore into the remote regions of the country. They entered the Beaver Valley the same day and stopped at a Native American town they called Coscosky, which was located about 1 mile below the junction of the Shenango and Mahoning Rivers where the Beaver River is formed. They doubtless followed the old Indian trail that began at what is now the west end of the Bridgewater Bridge, and continued up the west side of the Beaver to Kuskuskee.

In 1753, the French warned the tribes in this area that they were coming to build forts at Monongialo Forks (Pittsburgh), Logstown, and Beaver Creek. This aroused the English, and Governor Robert Dinwiddle of Virginia at once prepared an expedition to visit the scene. The governor appointed George Washington, then a youth of 22 years, to go with the party and ascertain the designs of the French. Washington undertook the mission on October 30, 1753 and came to Logstown, the most reliable point to make his inquiries. In Colonel Washington's journal of this expedition, he states that a party of the men at Logstown penetrated the Beaver Valley, and in all probability he was one of that party.

During the war between the French and English that followed, each nation was anxious to gain the confidence and support of the Indians as allies. To accomplish this purpose, on July 15, 1758, the English sent Christian Frederic Post, a Moravian from Philadelphia, to enlist the sympathy of the Native Americans. In the accomplishment of this mission, he passed through the Beaver Valley and stopped at a Native American town, which he called Kuskuskee. It contained 90 houses and 200 warriors of the Delaware tribe. It was the same place visited by Conrad Weiser, who had called it Coscosky.

On October 3, 1764, Colonel Henry Bouquet left Fort Pitt with a well-equipped army of 1,500 men to disperse the Indians who were desperate in their efforts to murder the whites. On his way to the Tuscarawas Valley, he passed through the Beaver Valley. The colonel spoke of the valley as very fertile and said that in getting across it they had to cross a very steep ridge.

In the year 1770, George Washington was again in the valley. In his journal, he made special mention of its fertility, attractiveness, and beauty, and said, "We came to the mouth of the Big Beaver Creek, opposite to which is a good situation for a house, etc." The "good situation" is now covered by the town of Monaca.

Thus far, all the expeditions had been military ones and while they were the only white men who had set foot in the valley, no permanent settlements were made until the 1770s. The valley had been overrun by military expeditions, but the Native American was yet the "monarch of all he surveyed."

A party of Moravians living on the Allegheny River made the first attempt at settlement. They had heard of the fertility of the Beaver Valley and the opportunity for doing well among the Indians, and left their homes on April 17, 1770 under the leadership of Reverend Daniel Zeisberger. The party arrived at the mouth of the Big Beaver on the forenoon of April 23 and rowed up the stream to the "falls." They had 16 canoes and at the falls they had to carry them and their baggage around the rapids, which took about five days. Parties from Kuskuskee met them here with horses and assisted them. They encamped on the east side of the Beaver near Kuskuskee on May 7 and established a settlement called Friedenstadt, or the "town of peace," about 1 mile below the "forks of the Beaver." This was the first permanent settlement of the whites in the valley.

This region attracted the attention of settlers and investors during the Revolutionary War. About 1779, General Daniel Broadhead, in command of the Western Department with headquarters at Fort Pitt, patented the lands on which Brighton was built. The lands were opposite the "middle falls" of the Beaver from where the dam at the 10th Street Bridge is now located and below. Broadhead was attracted by the waterpower possibility in the falls of the Beaver. The legislature of Pennsylvania passed a law on March 12, 1793, which opened up for sale and settlement the lands lying north of the Ohio and west of the Allegheny Rivers. General Daniel Broadhead applied at once for warrants for two tracts of 400 acres each, embracing the "black walnut bottoms" and all the land fronting on the middle falls. He had his land regularly entered, surveyed, and paid for with the intention of opening a settlement. Before he could accomplish this, the Indian

War of the Northwest broke out, preventing all settlements until the close of the war in 1795. The ravages of the war and Broadhead's advancing age prevented the general from making a personal settlement and the rich, desirable lands eventually fell into other, younger hands. This laid the foundations for a settlement that resulted in the busy and growing city of Beaver Falls.

Before the settlement of the lands of General Broadhead, Dr. Samuel Adams of Rowley, Massachusetts moved to the falls sometime before 1800 and settled at the "upper falls," which were called Adams Dam. He bought 400 acres of land extending from the present 17th Street to College Hill, and west including what is now known as Mt. Washington. Dr. Adams built a cabin near Eastvale Bridge and the upper dam, and had a gristmill and a sawmill. He and his son Milo were the only physicians on that side of Pittsburgh and were sent for from points 30 or 40 miles away. Samuel Adams was the first physician in the county and among the first—if not the first—settler on the site of Beaver Falls. He was also a local preacher in the Methodist Episcopal Church and held meetings at his home where as many as 40 or 50 people would be accommodated by him and his wife in their large house and barn. The place was known as Adamsville and is now a part of Beaver Falls. It antedated the town of Brighton by six or seven years.

John White, a native of Ireland, settled on what was known as the Platt Farm on the west side of town in 1793. A year later, he took land on the hill north of the present site of Geneva College. When Chippewa Township was divided into two townships, a decree was issued naming the new township "White" in honor of

MILO ADAMS. Milo Adams was the son of Dr. Samuel Adams and studied medicine under his father. His patient book from the early 1830s is on display at the Beaver Falls Museum.

PAPER MILL. This is the paper mill in Old Brighton, looking across the river from New Brighton. Notice the mill race from the dam powering the mill.

John White. His log cabin was located somewhere on present-day Ninth Street between Seventh and Eighth Avenues near the area of Lincoln Place. In August 1801, General Broadhead sold his two 400-acre tracts at the middle falls to David Hoopes of Chester County, Pennsylvania. Hoopes was a tanner by trade and, in 1766, married Esther Townsend, daughter of Joseph and Lydia Townsend of East Bradford in Chester County. They moved to Brighton in 1802. Among their children was Joseph, born October 28, 1770, who was the father of Edward Hoopes, born December 18, 1800 in Wilmington, Delaware. Edward came to Brighton with his parents when he was two years old and later became the progenitor of the Hoopes family of lower Third Avenue, New Brighton.

David Hoopes bought these desirable tracts for the use of Hoopes, Townsend and Company and paid $3,000 for the land. The Hoopes intended to utilize the site for the superior waterpower afforded by the location at the falls. When David Hoopes came from Chester County to take charge of his purchase, he found several settlers on the land who were claiming it under the provision of the law of 1792 relating to securing title by "settlement and improvement." General Broadhead had instituted suits in the United States courts and had secured judgments in his favor, but Hoopes had trouble with them and had to buy some of the property from the settlers.

Hoopes, Townsend and Company erected a sawmill, which burned a short time later, but was rebuilt. Afterward, it was increased in size by the addition of a flourmill, the second of its kind at the falls. Across the river, at the New Brighton end of the present 10th Street Bridge, John Wolf erected a flour mill in 1799, which was the first mill in the county east of the Beaver.

Sometime in 1804, the company began the erection of a forge on the river a short distance above their mills, but before the work was completed, the property passed into the possession of Isaac Wilson in 1805. The forge was completed and began operations in 1806. Mr. Wilson also built a charcoal furnace, but before its completion, he sold a half interest in the entire plant to Barker & Gregg for $16,000 on September 13, 1808. The new firm was known as Isaac Wilson and Company. Toward the close of 1808, the firm completed a blast furnace and for several years actively engaged in making iron, stoves, hollow-ware, etc. using the kidney ore found on the ground. In April 1812, Barker & Gregg purchased Isaac Wilson's half interest for $15,000.

Sometime later, Frederick Rapp of the Harmony Society tried to purchase the entire plant with the improvements, but was unsuccessful because of the doubts over the titles. The property came into the possession of Oliver Ormsby of Allegheny County who continued all the operations under the supervision of James Glenn and Colonel John Dickey until 1818. Due to the slow down in business because of the war with England, the works lost much business and the growth of the town was stalled. It remained this way until the depression ended in 1829.

Improvements were also being made during this period at the lower falls of the Beaver at what is now Fallston. On June 19, 1799, David Townsend purchased a 100-acre tract of land on this site from John McKee. The property was then sold to a company composed of David Townsend, Benjamin Townsend, and Benjamin Sharpless. On December 3, 1802, one-third of the land was sold to Evan and John Pugh. In 1800, David Townsend started a sawmill. In 1804, the Pughs started a flour mill and in 1808, David Townsend started a mill to make linseed oil and another mill for the manufacture and spinning of cottons. In 1809, Septimus Sharpless started a wool mill and in 1812, James Douglass started a mill to make carding machines. In 1823, Marsh & Stone started a place to manufacture scythes and in 1823, William Eichlaum started a paper mill. In 1825, John and Evan Pugh, Hall Wilson, and Thomas Thonily started a cotton factory and in 1826, John Milner, M.F. Champlin, W. Porter, and B.F. Mathers started a bucket factory which two years later was known as the Darragh Machine Shop. In 1828, Robert Townsend, Reese C. Townsend, and Baird & Company started the wire and rivet mill. These were some of the early industries in the area of that one tract of land. Brighton and Fallston were the prominent manufacturing locations at the falls of the Beaver. New Brighton did not enter into manufacturing until around 1836 and Fallston was by then in the lead.

The name Brighton was given to the town at the middle falls in 1806. The interesting history that is connected with the town is as follows. In 1803, Hoopes, Townsend and Company erected a building in Sharon, now the upper part of Bridgewater. It was the second house from Brady's Run and was used for merchandising by Isaac Wilson who came from Chester County, Pennsylvania.

Wilson was the grandfather of Wade Wilson of New Brighton and was a prominent factor in the building of the valley. The building was called the "Old Red Front." Near this old building on the flat between the river and Brady's Run, in 1806, Aaron Burr's managers and workmen built a flotilla of boats as a part of his expedition down the Ohio to found his new empire. Amasa Brown of Utica, New York, grandfather of the Honorable Hartford P. Brown of Rochester, was the superintendent or master boat builder. The boats were 60 to 70 feet in length, similar in style to the old keelboats, but covered closely and made waterproof. The workmen were lodged in a house next to the "Old Red Front." With this expedition were two English brothers named Constable whose descendants were prominent in New York City. They had no part in the expedition, but went along merely to see the country and sketch its interesting points. The owners of the "black walnut bottoms" at the middle falls wished to lay out a plan of lots and engaged the Constable brothers, who were engineers, for the job. They agreed to do the work with the condition that they be allowed to name the town. This was agreed to and when the surveying was finished, they named the town "Brighton" after their old home in England.

The reason for the place being known many years later as "Old Brighton" and the change to its being called Beaver Falls is no less curious than its original naming. In 1815, a plan of lots was laid out in what is now New Brighton, the part between Fifth Avenue and the Beaver River, at the upper end, on tract number 94. By an Act of Assembly on March 20, 1810, a company was incorporated under the name of "The President, Managers & Company for erecting a bridge over Big Beaver Creek opposite the town of Brighton," where the present bridge is at the upper end of Third Avenue, New Brighton. By erecting the bridge where it was laid out, neither end would be "opposite the town of Brighton" as a township lay between the western end of the proposed bridge and the town of Brighton at the middle falls. To overcome this and conform to the charter, it was decided to call the new town on the eastern side of the river "East Brighton," and thus the eastern end of the bridge was "opposite the town of (East) Brighton." When the new town was incorporated in 1838, it was called "New Brighton," and the earlier town was generally called "Old Brighton" until it was changed to Beaver Falls in 1867. Joseph Hoopes was the surveyor and J. Webster Wilson, father of Wade Wilson, was the chain carrier. The original plot is still in the possession of J. Webster Wilson. The family of the late Joseph L. Pugh of lower Third Avenue, New Brighton, has the bill of sale of these lots.

The revival of the industries in Brighton began in 1829 when James Patterson appeared on the scene and purchased the interests of Oliver Ormsby, securing in all about 1,300 acres. Patterson was a man of strong character and iron will, and he put all his energy into whatever he undertook. He was a native of Ireland, coming with his parents to Albany, New York where he remained until early manhood. He then went to Philadelphia where he manufactured tanks for several years. Afterward, he erected a cotton mill at Doe Run in Chester County, remaining in business until he settled at Brighton.

BRIGHTON MILLS. This is an advertising card from James Patterson's Brighton Mills, which included a flour mill, a cotton mill, and a sawmill. Old Brighton never developed above Eighth Street.

Patterson brought his family and some machinery with him and began to improve the property, building a flour mill with a capacity of 200 barrels a day, and a cotton factory that employed 35 hands and yielded 3,000 pounds of yarn per week. He also started a copper shop on the site of Mayer Brothers Pottery and all these businesses were on the bank of the river below the dam at the second falls. These enterprises were a great factor in reviving trade and circulating money throughout the country in exchange for wheat, wool, and other commodities. Patterson had a good deal of trouble in securing titles to his purchases on account of General Broadhead being compelled to enter suits to perfect his titles to the lands that were not finally settled until 1865, when the United States Supreme Court decided in Patterson's favor. He seems to have expended much of his means and energy in gaining title to his property, which was a detriment to business. He left a large family, many of his descendants being the most prominent men in the county.

In 1829, Archibald Robertson also came to the place and began an active and useful career in helping to add to the industries of the town. He was born in County Tyrone, Ireland on March 5, 1803, and came to this country with his parents in 1812. He was one of the thousands of Scotch-Irish who added not only to the industries, but also to the character of western Pennsylvania. Robertson became interested in a paper mill in Fallston in 1828 and, in 1829, he built a steam paper mill at what is now the corner of Ninth Avenue and Fifth Street in Beaver

Falls, the site now occupied by the freight station of the Pennsylvania Lines. He operated this mill successfully for about 20 years. Robertson made an excellent quality of wallpaper and printing paper, employed a considerable number of hands, including about a dozen families, and did much for the business interests of the town. In 1843, the *Beaver Argus* used the paper made by this mill for its issues and copies still in existence show the paper to be in excellent condition, still holding its color much better than the ordinary printing paper of the present.

The Middle Falls of the Beaver were now assuming much importance, but not as much perhaps as they would have had the United States government secured control of them as was desired. In 1822, government engineers were sent to examine the waterpower afforded by the several falls of the Big Beaver, with the view of establishing a national armory. The report of the engineers favored the site and the outlook was quite good for the erection of the armory, but other localities were also after it and the opposition became so formidable that it was lost.

In the year 1833, Marcus T.C. Gould came to New Brighton from Rome, New York and established the New Brighton Female Seminary. He was a remarkable character and had great influence in the valley. Gould had unbounded faith in the future of the falls of the Beaver and constructed a map taking in all of the Beaver Valley to the vicinity of Darlington, which he called "Beaver City." He used this name in correspondence with the Pittsburgh Board of Trade to call attention to the advantage of the valley and its surroundings. Gould was regarded by many of the people as a visionary who evidently had a prophetic spirit. In a letter written

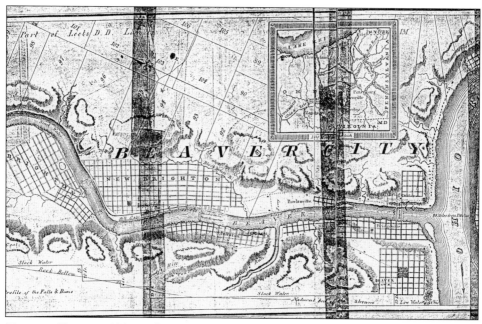

BEAVER VALLEY, 1836. This map shows the location of Adamsville, Brighton, New Brighton, and other towns in the valley.

by him in December 1835 to Atkinson's Casket, Philadelphia, he made the following prediction:

> I now predict, through this epistle that within ten years from this time, there will be a population of at least 20,000 about the falls and mouth of the Beaver. Nor would we in the slightest degree insinuate that any future benefits which the falls of the Beaver may derive, will detract from the growth or prosperity of Pittsburgh, but on the contrary. I am proud to consider the falls of the Beaver as a suburb of that immense city which is soon to be the wonder of the Western World——place to which this and almost every other place within hundreds of miles must in some respects pay tribute. We shall not be long behind any other towns west of the Allegheny Mountains, for the variety, quality and extent of our manufactures. (Pittsburgh excepted) We shall not long hear the inquiry, where is Brighton? Where is Fallston? Where are the Falls of Beaver? Where is Beaver County, Pennsylvania?

These predictions did not come true within the time set because of several factors, but in due time they have come true and now the Falls of the Beaver and vicinity within the range of Gould's map has a population of between 40,000 and 50,000 people.

Business was fair in Brighton at about the time Gould was making his predictions and gradual improvement was being made, but the panic of 1837 gave the place another set-back that halted progress for some years.

A boom came in New Brighton when a branch of the United States bank was established, which affected the whole area.

In the charter of the Bank of Pennsylvania, under the influence of the Honorable John Dickey, it was stipulated that the bank might establish branches, "one of which must be in Beaver County." Taking advantage of this, the bank established a branch at New Brighton with the following officers: president, John Pugh; cashier, Dr. William Dent; directors, Robert Townsend, M.F. Champlin, James Patterson, Ovid Pinney, Dr. E.K. Chamberlin, A.W. Townsend, and J.P. Johnston, all of Beaver County; John B. Pearson of Mercer County; and John Gilmore of Butler County. All responsible persons were urged to borrow money, which increased the volume of business in the community. This came at a fearful cost when settlement time came. Bank obligations had to be met, the mother bank in Philadelphia failed and a financial panic followed, causing disaster and ruin. Values were depressed, property had no sale value and the effect on the community was disastrous. Afterwards, a large amount of the debts were compromised, by which most of the manufacturers were enabled, in a small way at least, to resume business and in time confidence was restored.

This bank in New Brighton was at what is now 1307 Third Avenue, a one-story building. The neighborhood was much affected and it was years before the ill effects passed away.

The first post office established in the place was called Brighton and was opened in 1818 and continued until 1857. The postmasters were as follows with the date of appointment of each: John Dickey, April 11, 1818; David Hoopes, May 17, 1821; James Patterson, December 26, 1832; Archibald Robertson, February 8, 1843; Matthew H. Robertson, December 19, 1850; and James B. McCallan, June 19, 1856.

The old two-room brick schoolhouse on Seventh Avenue near Eighth Street was the only public building in Brighton and was used for all public meetings, etc. Here school was held, the first report of which was made to the enlarged town in 1867. This was the only school building prior to the incorporation of Beaver Falls, and the only place in which religious meetings could be held until the erection of the Presbyterian and Methodist Episcopal Churches, both of which were built after the organization of the new borough.

Many of the boys and girls of Brighton attended a young ladies' seminary conducted by a Miss Curtis in New Brighton on the corner of 1311 Third Avenue. Curtis employed an able corps of accomplished and refined young women teachers and contributed largely to the uplifting of character. Although a New Brighton institution, her pupils were drawn from the valley towns as well as from a distance. While it was primarily a young ladies seminary, boys were received as day scholars, and how she drilled her lads in patriotism and love of country! It was all vividly recalled during the Spanish War when harking back to the early 1850s, as old pupils recalled Curtis holding up her hands in horror recounting the deeds of the blood-thirsty Spaniards in their wars of conquest, contrasting this with the lofty patriotism of Washington. And in later years, no region in the country sent more good soldiers to the field than our own valley towns. No doubt much of it was due to the patriotic teachings of that woman.

The first newspaper in the town of Brighton was called the *Beaver Falls Chronicle*. This paper was the successor of the *Aurora*, which was discontinued on March 1, 1839. The *Beaver Falls Chronicle* began its existence at Rochester on October 12, 1839, with J. Washington White, the last editor of the *Aurora*, as editor. The motto of the paper was "Our country right or wrong." It was a four-page, six-column paper and the amount of reading matter would compare favorably with many of the weeklies of today. The paper suspended for some time in early 1840, the following reference being made to it by the *Argus* of March 11, 1840:

> A number of the "Beaver Falls Chronicle" which had been suspended for some weeks, was issued a few days ago. The editor gives good reasons for his suspension and takes occasion to lash the Loco Foci leaders with great severity. He has been shamefully treated by professional friends who led him into difficulty and took advantage of his situation.

In June 1840, the *Chronicle* hauled down the Van Buren flag and enlisted under the banner of Harrison for president and was thereafter a Whig paper. It remained in Rochester until July 1840. In its issue of July 23, the following editorial notice appeared:

> The office of the "Beaver Falls Chronicle" has been removed from Rochester to Brighton. Those of our subscribers who reside in Rochester and its vicinity will find their papers by calling at Jacob Hinds grocery—those in Beaver can call at the book store of J. Bowen—those of Fallston, at Mr. Cannon's store and those in New Brighton, at the store of Mr. Hoopes.

This closed the career of the paper as a Rochester institution.

On August 29, 1840, J. Washington White, editor and proprietor of the *Beaver Falls Chronicle*, formally transferred the paper to E. Burk Fisher with the following notice:

> With the last number of the "Beaver Falls Chronicle" the subscriber relinquished his connection with it, and has signed the establishment to E. Burk Fisher, Esq., who will hereafter publish it under the title of "Beaver Falls Palladium." In introducing his successor to the confidence of his old subscribers, the subscriber feels that the name of Mr. Fisher

LOWER BEAVER FALLS. Notice that houses have been built on Bridge Street; also, Beaver Valley Glass Plant has been built. The Beaver Valley Glass Plant later becomes the Whitla Glass Company, which burned in 1892.

BEAVER FALLS, 1869. This is the lower end of town. Notice that no houses have been built on Bridge Street and the Black Horse Tavern is still standing between the covered bridge and the railroad bridge.

> will be sufficient guarantee that the character of the "Palladium" will be fully commensurate with the interests and wishes of Beaver County. Mr. Fisher has been a publisher for more than ten years, and must be well known to the citizens of this county.

Fisher came from Pittsburgh where he edited the *Literary Examiner and Western Monthly Review* and was also editor of the *Saturday Evening Visitor*. Fisher took charge of the paper, promising to publish a clean, decent paper that "will never be the vehicle of falsehood or assailant of individual reputation." After defending his political standing, he said the following:

> When the heat of the political excitement shall have been lost in the result of the approaching contest, and our duty as a politician shall for the time be suspended, it will afford him pleasure to assume the less exciting, but equally grateful duty of a herald of the business resources of Beaver County.

He espoused the cause of General Harrison and placed at the head of his paper the motto: "Take away the sword—the pen can save the state," an exclamation attributed to Richelleu, whom Fisher made the subject of a two-column article, political to the core. The paper was published at $2 per annum and was the same size as its predecessor. The September 1840 issue of his paper contained nine columns of sheriff's sales, signed by David Somers, sheriff. It also contained three columns of ordinances of New Brighton Borough, signed by Harvey Blanchard, president of council, and Harvey Thomas, clerk.

From the time of assuming charge of the paper until the national election, Fisher made as red hot a political paper as the country could produce. In its issue of October 29, he had an editorial entitled, "The Editor to His Fellow Citizens," which was more than five columns in length, a "last word" that was full of political vim. From December 12, 1840, the name of E.B. Fisher disappeared from the paper and the prospectus was signed "Publisher of Beaver County Palladium." In the issue of December 26, 1840, the following was printed in the paper:

> Take notice that we have applied to the Judge of the Court of Common Pleas, of Beaver County, for the relief provided for insolvent debtors, by the law of the Commonwealth of Pennsylvania, and that they have appointed the first Monday of March next, for the hearing of us and our creditors, at the Court House in the borough of Beaver, at which time and place you may attend if you think proper. E.B. Fisher, W.H. Whitney, late printers.

On February 6, 1841, the firm of William H. Eskridge and Company appeared at the head of the paper, which disappeared after the issue of March 12. The motto was changed to "The Throne We Honor is the People's Choice."

On March 10, 1841, the name of John B. Early appeared as editor. In his prospectus, he said that, "at the solicitation of a number of friends, he has consented once more to assume the arduous duties of a newspaper editor." While continuing the paper as a supporter of President Harrison's administration, he wrote: "Its columns shall be free from those foul blots of party malevolence and personal detraction, which instead of being productive of good, are calculated to sow the seeds of embittered dissension, and pander to the worst passions of human nature." Early made a good paper, which was fairly well patronized with advertisements, but it was doubtless too expensive for the population, and was discontinued in the fall of 1841. No record exists of any other paper in the town until 1874.

The First Presbyterian Church was organized in 1867. Previous to that time, irregular services were held by Presbyterians in the town in the old school building, and on May 1, 1866, a union Sunday school was started with 30 scholars. In 1867, application was made to the Presbytery for an organization, and on November 22, a committee was appointed by that body to organize a church if the way should be clear. The committee organized a church with 25 members, with the ruling elders William Frazier, A.C. Thorue, and W.W. Parkinson. In the spring of 1868, the Reverend Albert Dillworth was settled as the first regular pastor and in 1869, a church building was erected.

In 1867, the Reverend J.J. McIlyar, pastor of the New Brighton Methodist Episcopal Church, held services in the schoolhouse and the following winter, revival meetings were held, resulting in a number of accessions to the church. In the spring of 1868, the Harmony Society donated two lots and loaned the church $2,000 and they erected a church, which McIlyar supplied until the Reverend B.F. Sawhill was appointed to the pastorate.

Following the depression in Brighton after the panic of 1837, there was not much business in its later history. Harris's Pittsburgh Business Directory for 1841 gives the following exhibit of the place:

> The two leading manufacturing interests, it may be well inferred, were those of Patterson and Robertson, Patterson's flouring mill was capable of turning out 200 barrels of flour per day. The flour was of superior quality, being adjudged in Philadelphia; whither it was principally shipped, equal to the best Genessee brand. During the navigable season three boats were in demand to supply the necessary quantity of wheat. The mill required six hands, and the shops gave employment to sixteen coopers.

The cotton mill under Patterson's direction employed 35 hands and yielded 8,000 pounds of yarn per week. The steam paper mill owned by Archibald Robertson required four engines. Connected with it was a staining establishment, which gave employment to ten families.

The school directors of the town were Robert Calhoun, John Baker, Thomas D. Wells, James M. Gregg, James Patterson, and A. Robertson.

The various industries were thus represented: laborers—David Ames, Jeremiah Maid, Emory Maloy; millwright—James B. Angel; papermakers—John Baker, James C. Fulton, James Roberts, H. Woods, Jessie Zeigler; innkeepers—Luke Bland, Widow Sutliff; blacksmiths—David Bolles, William J. King; farmers—John Bolles, Robert McGaughey; engineers—William Carter, Daniel Loomis; carpenters—Robert Calhoun, Joseph Reeves; calico printer—William Clayton; clerks—J.K. Dean, C.H. Gould, William Harrison; coal diggers—Charles Day, Nathan Dillon; machinists—James M. Greig and James Wilson; canal boat captain—George Hemphill; tanner—John R. Hoopes; foreman flouring mill—H. Huggins; sign painter—Samuel Kenedy; cabinet makers—Horatio Large, H. Sims Sr., H. Sims Jr.; forgeman—John Martin, James Richards; tailors—Ephriam Martin, William Wallace; brick maker—Robert Moffit; teamsters—Joseph Mahaffee, John Murrell; cooper—Peter W. Maltby; foreman cotton factory—Andrew Nelson; storekeeper and flour merchant—James Patterson; shoemaker—William B. Platt; wheat agent—Ira Ransom; paper mill owner—Archibald Robertson; soap manufacturer—Isaac Warren; saddler—David Whitla.

In addition to the foregoing, between 1841 and the establishment of Beaver Falls, Thomas Hennon was a wagon builder; John Sims, cabinet maker on Water Street; Thomas Hillier, brickyard, Seventh Street between Seventh and Eighth Avenues as now laid out; James Renton operated the old furnace on the ground

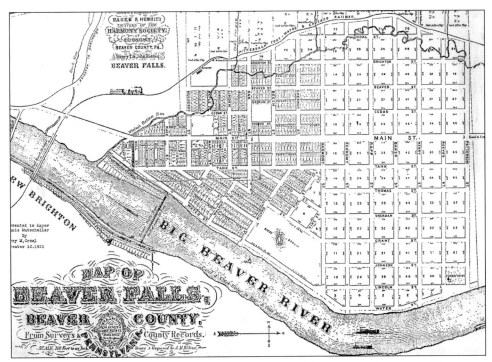

LAYOUT OF BEAVER FALLS, 1866. Notice the names of the streets and avenues. The names were changed to the current system for better mail delivery.

on which the Cutlery was built later, which went out of blast finally in 1854 and 1855.

During the ownership of the lands here by James Patterson, he plotted a town July 4, 1849, the plan being acknowledged before William Richardson, J.P., on August 4. The names of the streets starting with the river were Tank, Main, and Cedar; and those at right angles with the latter were Factory, Mill, Race, Mulberry, Linden, and Oak.

In 1849, Archibald Robertson built a paper mill to be operated by waterpower at the head of the falls, then called Adamsville, which he owned and operated until 1864 when he sold out to the Pittsburg Manufacturing Company. It was in operation for many years after that by Frazier, Metzgar and Company.

In the early 1850s, Marcus T.C. Gould promoted the Beaver Manufacturing Company, which interested eastern capital. The following gentlemen composed the company: John Thompson, Turner Truesdale, John Newbold, and Walter Chester. This company operated the Patterson Industries for a few years, and cut a considerable figure in the valley for some years, but the business depression culminating in the panic of 1857 swept them off their feet. The Pittsburgh, Fort Wayne & Chicago Railroad was completed through the valley in 1852 and was a splendid outlet for Brighton, but failed to add to or increase the industries of the town at that time.

After the destruction of the arsenal at Harper's Ferry in 1861, efforts were made in the two sessions of the Congress in 1861–1862 and 1862–1863 to have the government purchase the property at Brighton for a National Armory, but to no purpose, and Rock Island, Illinois was selected instead.

The Harmony Society held several mortgages on the property and purchased it at sheriff's sale for the sum of $34,500. In 1866, the society made a new survey of the town, revising the plot and greatly enlarging it, with a view of establishing a large town. It was extended along the Beaver River about 3 miles, and the society began to actively forward the interests of the place. They appointed Henry T. and John Reeves, known as H.T. & J. Reeves, real estate agents, to offer the lots for sale.

The Reeves family was among the earliest settlers of Brighton. Daniel Reeves, born at Mount Holly, New Jersey in 1785, father of Henry T. Reeves and John Reeves, came to Brighton in 1805 and was a cabinetmaker and carpenter until his death on December 1, 1837. John Reeves was born February 9, 1825 and Henry T. Reeves on October 14, 1827. In the year 1856, the two brothers engaged in merchandising in New Brighton. They disposed of their business in 1865 and engaged in real estate operations. Their history in business was a part of that of Beaver Falls.

Robertson was appointed collector of Internal Revenue of the 24th District of Pennsylvania in October 1866 and retired from the office in May 1869. He was a

COVERED BRIDGE. *This is the Beaver Falls entrance to the covered bridge between Beaver Falls and New Brighton. Notice the streetcar tracks crossing the bridge.*

member of the state senate in 1851 and 1852, representing the district composed of Beaver, Butler, and Lawrence Counties and was quite prominent in the politics of his county. He was an old-school gentleman of a pleasant manner and disposition and was held in high esteem by his neighbors. His son Lieutenant Commander James P. Robertson of the U.S. Navy was born on December 18, 1840 and entered the U.S. Naval Academy on September 25, 1857. In May 1861, he was assigned to Admiral Dupont's flagship the *Wabash*, his first battle being at Port Royal. He was promoted to lieutenant commander on August 16, 1866.

William Robertson held an important position in his father's office and was one of the party of young men who helped pave the way for the future Beaver Falls. Robertson lived on his farm back of New Brighton where he and his son were associated in the business of mining the Trough Run "fire clay." He won his spurs in the business world in the chain business, being the treasurer of the Standard Chain Company of Pittsburgh. It was an important position, which he filled with great ability.

Among the others in the office for some time was Charles Baker, son of John Baker, brother-in-law of Archibald Robertson and Ira D. Sankey whose genial presence was always enjoyed by the office. Robertson's office was in the old homestead at the corner of Seventh Avenue and Fifth Street, which was occupied years later by Dr. W.H. Grim, who married Robertson's daughter. A vast amount of business was done in this office, covering the counties of Beaver, Lawrence, Washington, and Greene.

In those olden days, there were not many people in the town, but much was made of the society Beaver Falls had in connection with the people of New Brighton. Henry T. Reeves and a number of others used to hold prayer meetings in the old schoolhouse, Reeves being a leader in that work and much respected by his younger associates, who aided materially in the development of the church life and in erecting churches.

In addition to the families already named, there were a number of others who were prominent in all social affairs and later in business activities. They became very much interested when the Harmony Society planned extensive industrial movements, and the feeling was common that a great future awaited the town. In the early part of 1867, a debating society held forth in the old schoolhouse and the discussions were certainly lively enough and of considerable ability in the treatment of public questions.

Those who were present would remember one paper in particular, prepared and read by Charles Taylor. It was known that the writer of the paper had a fertile imagination, but it was not supposed that he had the prophetic gift. The paper was devoted to the industrial and business future of the newly awakened town. It pictured in glowing colors the rise of the town to greatness, huge factories along the river employing large numbers of workmen, warehouses of great magnitude and mammoth proportions, streets lined with business houses, beautiful homes, fine churches, and commodious schoolhouses, well kept streets and a happy, thriving people in a bustling and beautiful city.

In a general way, the prediction had been fulfilled and if anything, the growing, prosperous borough exceeds in importance what the vivid imagination of the writer so graphically foretold. But he was not alone in his views, for others foretold what they believed was sure to come, and when the Reeves Real Estate Agency got down to business and put lots on the market, then things began to move. Seventh Avenue lots below the hill sold rapidly and at fair prices and purchasers secured what turned out to be good bargains. Manufacturers appeared on the scene and secured locations, merchants began to figure on eligible sites, churches were to the front for choice lots, and there was bustle and activity all along the line.

The town started off with a rush under the stimulus of the Harmony Society, which began to carry on and aid various manufacturing and other enterprises. The only new works that had a fair start in the old town under the new auspices was the Cutlery Company, whose operations began in 1868. The Howard Stove Works was started in 1868 by A.F. Wolf, and in the fall of that year, Isaac A. Harvey made Liverpool ware on the site of the Art Tile Company, Elijah Webster had stoneware pottery succeeding Chapman and Company on the site of the Mayer Brothers Pottery, which passed into the hands of the Harmony Society, but they came rapidly enough after that. The Economy Savings Institution was started in March 1868 with Henry Hice as its president.

One of the most capable young men of the town was Thomas R. Hennon, son of John Hennon, who was associated for many years with the Harmony Society in its oil and lumber business up the Allegheny River and later in the management of the Economy Savings Institution.

The town grew rapidly in population and business and in 1868, the citizens felt that they should be incorporated as a borough. This was done by a decree of the court on November 9, 1868, and the name changed to Beaver Falls, to obviate the confusion between the old name of "Brighton" and New Brighton on the opposite side of the river. Beaver Falls was also the natural name of the place. The first paper in the town in 1840 was called the *Beaver Falls Chronicle*, and this section of the valley and about Fallston was known as Beaver Falls in the early part of the century. The later history of the place after November 9, 1868 comes under the head of Beaver Falls, a thriving third-class city of probably 15,000 people.

2. THE CITY GROWS

Sometime around the year 1804, mail was brought into this area, probably by coach and horseback to the Blackhorse Inn, which was located in the vicinity of the present Union Drawn Division of Republic Steel's office building. It was not really a post office, but sort of an unofficial area center for travelers, mail, and news. This is how mail was handled locally for almost a century before regular postal service was instituted.

The first formal post office in what was to become Beaver Falls was established April 11, 1818, in a store owned by John Dickey, the first postmaster. The settlement then was known as Brighton and later as Old Brighton.

On May 17, 1821, David Hoopes became postmaster. James Patterson, most prominent in early town history, took over December 25, 1832. Archibald Robertson became postmaster on February 8, 1843 and during his term (in 1847), the use of prepayment of postage by affixed stamps was initiated. Mathew A. Robertson succeeded him on December 19, 1850 and Joseph McClellan became postmaster on June 19, 1856.

Early in 1857, Moses Knott, father of James W. Knott of Knott and Harker Company, bought a small store next door to his home at 618 Sixth Street. This store was the site of the village post office, so he automatically became postmaster (which at this time appeared to be the customary procedure).

On April 24, 1857, the Brighton post office was closed. It is reported that at this time, postal business was very slight. It wasn't always that way.

While Moses Knott was postmaster, a very big social event occurred. D. O'Connel Patterson (son of James Patterson, early settler and influential citizen) married Elvira Dickey. On the day the invitations to his wedding were mailed, the mail volume happened to be big—so big the store was closed and only the post office was in operation.

On July 4, 1867, the "post office" was re-established as Beaver Falls. The type of post office setup used then is still found in small communities today. A prototype may be observed at Old Economy in Ambridge.

In 1867, the general store of Dawson and Richardson on the northwest corner of Seventh Avenue and Third Street under the postmaster-ship of Edward A. Noble was the base of postal operations. On February 11, 1869, under Milo A.

NEW POST OFFICE, 1938. This photograph shows the dedication of the new post office on the corner of Eighth Avenue and 11th Street.

Townsend, it was moved to a print shop on the east side of Seventh Avenue between Third and Fourth Streets. It was later moved to the Reeves building at 333 Seventh Avenue. It again moved to 701 Seventh Avenue, a brick building, gradually "drifting" northward toward today's main business section.

In December 1872, Joseph L.B. Dawson became postmaster and, for the first time in Beaver Falls, the post office was separate from other businesses. Dawson leased a storeroom from Hanovers on the east side of the 600 block of Seventh Avenue; then in 1878, he moved to a small frame building at 927 Seventh Avenue. Next came Samuel S. McFerron, who on January 14, 1881, became what a report published in *The News-Tribune's* 75th anniversary edition called the first official postmaster. William A. Grim was appointed on February 28, 1889 and on February 6, 1893, Harry F. Hawkins was appointed. City delivery of mail was inaugurated in the spring of 1889 under Grim. Five carriers were appointed. During Hawkins's term as postmaster, a federal post office building was constructed at 13th Street and Seventh Avenue. This was in use from October 1897 until November 1938.

William T. Levis took over July 1, 1930, the year Beaver Falls became a third-class city and annexed College Hill. The Beaver Falls Post Office always served College Hill. On July 16, 1934, Robert W. Baggs was appointed and served until his retirement in June 1965. Baggs not only served the longest tenure as postmaster in the history of the Beaver Falls office, but was also the only one to terminate his tenure by official retirement. It was during Baggs's postmaster-ship that the post office building at 11th Street and Eighth Avenue was built. It was dedicated in 1938.

Since its inception, the Beaver Falls Police Department has earned the reputation of being one of the finest, most efficient law enforcement units in the entire state of Pennsylvania. Over the years, it has acquired a colorful history of dedicated service and outstanding accomplishments.

Many of its members have been killed, wounded, or injured while performing their duty. They have participated in most conceivable types of criminal activity. Beaver Falls has handled and solved murder cases, armed robberies, kidnappings, hostage situations, drug traffic, and any other type of incident the criminal element can engage in.

The police have won many awards for their actions, received both state and federal recognition, plus many certificates, proclamations, and medals for outstanding heroic action. The Beaver Falls police department has earned the respect and gratitude of the local residents.

During the 1800s, what was then considered Old Brighton was still generally large tracts of wilderness area populated by settlers and a few isolated merchants. Crime was practically unheard of in those more innocent times and there was no organized police force, just a single peace officer. Whatever justice needed to be enforced was usually done privately or with community consent. But during that period, years could pass without any incident of a criminal nature.

Beaver Falls borough at that time was a rural area in a nation of farmers. A man's word was his bond and being a good supportive neighbor was the normal, accepted way of life. Hard work, love of family, dedication, and determination along with a firm religious foundation was the creed and motto of every family.

Whatever crime existed came in the form of habitual drunkards or someone having a little too much to drink over the weekend. There might be an occasional small theft or perhaps a horse theft, which was a serious crime, but by and large those were the only crimes during those oh-so-innocent times.

It was during 1879 that the presiding burgher A.G. McCreary was empowered to hire three persons as official police. But only two were initially hired. They were J.P. McGown and John Elliot. These two men were forever enshrined in city history as the first paid law enforcement officers. However, they were quickly let go the following year and replaced by Robert Conkle, John Davis, and Charles Patterson. These men were paid $1.50 for each arrest made.

Beaver Falls at this point consisted of only a few streets. The main avenue was still an earthen thoroughfare. Horses, buggies, and wagons were the modes of transportation and the new patrolling police officers were occasionally mounted as they made their daily patrols. There was a swine pen located next to the lockup, which held pigs that were caught running loose on the streets.

New policemen were appointed every year until 1890. They were non-uniformed and carried a mace or nightstick as a weapon. Weekends that usually resulted in some rowdiness required the officers to patrol the streets until 12 p.m. on Saturdays. During these times, an officer's word was law and the first lawmen were tough and hard and would not tolerate any foolishness or back talk. A policeman was to be respected and listened to.

The first elected law officer in 1868 was Squire C.W. Taylor. The high constable J. Hickman was the chief arresting officer for a number of years. As a matter of fact, at times he was the only officer except for Williams Rea, who was employed as the engine house janitor.

It was in 1872 that citizens petitioned council to hire paid full-time policemen, which council did by authorizing burgher McCreary to hire two Pittsburgh policemen for four months at only $50 per month.

Thomas Gelston was hired in 1873 to oversee the department at a salary of $85. These policemen were all later dismissed and a former councilman, James Crane, was hired at $2 a day and, as far as can be ascertained, was the first city policeman given permission to carry a revolver. One of Crane's duties in 1874 was to light the newly installed gas lamps on the city streets. For the next several years, special police were hired in the summers only because of disorderly picnics and more street traffic.

The former borough building was constructed in 1880. The jail was adjacent to the borough building and during these times, if anyone was arrested, the prisoner was given only bread, cheese, and water, which were purchased from the J.H. Brackens Hotel.

City records show that former sheriff and high constable Chamberlain White, a large, powerful man who epitomized authority, became Beaver Falls chief of police in 1879 and continued in that capacity until 1888. In 1884, White was both police chief and health officer with a wage of $50 per month.

Because of severe unrest due to strikes at the Hartman Steel Company wire and nail mill that created much tension and street fighting, council was again petitioned for more permanent police protection. On July 19, 1884, a police force was established with six properly uniformed men complete with long, dark blue double-breasted coats, helmets, and maces. Today we refer to these uniforms as "Keystone Cop" outfits, but at the time, this was the standard, officially recognized police uniform. Thus Beaver Falls at last had a professional looking police force. The men were Chief Chamberlain White, Dennis McAuliffe, Phillip Crawl, Wilson Cunningham, David R. Porter, Abe Wolf, and William Rae. Rae was still the City Building janitor as well as an acting day policeman.

The department was now formally organized with two permanent night policemen at $40 a month. The uniform cost $29.50 complete, which the men paid for themselves. If they remained on the force long enough, they would eventually be reimbursed.

In 1884, George King of 1021 Fourth Avenue was the first black police officer in Beaver Falls. Thus, Beaver Falls can attest with pride that not only was it among the very first western Pennsylvania police departments to hire a black officer, but was also among the first in the entire nation.

The first officer killed in the line of duty was W.T. Tully, who was chief at the time. He died during an accident that occurred at the 22nd Street underpass in 1918.

The number of officers employed continued to fluctuate at the turn of the century and into the early 1900s. This was due to the economics of the times plus the fact that rampant crime was hardly in evidence. This was a time of gas lit street lamps with residents going to bed at early hours. The streets were practically deserted by 8 p.m. Theft, rowdiness, and drunkenness were about the only crimes and even they seldom occurred. The officers patrolled up and down the city streets, familiar, respected figures of authority to all. They were easily recognized and residents knew each individual officer, feeling safe and comfortable.

It was a time when an officer could cuff a youngster's ears for misbehaving, knowing the parent would do the same. The frequent use of a nightstick to emphasize a point was also employed and a policeman wasn't afraid to use his strength and muscle to subdue a wrongdoer.

By 1909, the force had grown to 12 men and during the 1910s and 1930s, it eventually rose to 20 men. Up until the mid-1900s, police officers would still occasionally patrol on horseback and the paddy wagon, or the infamous "Black

POLICE DEPARTMENT, 1900s. Our finest pose in their dress uniforms, what we commonly call Keystone Cop Uniforms, named after the early silent movie comedies.

Morai" as it was termed, was still horse-drawn. It wasn't until late 1910 that motor vehicles were obtained for the force.

Early records show that the first speeding violation was in April 1910, which resulted in a $10 fine and $2 in court costs. The first stolen car was reported in 1918 when a Ford touring car was absconded with. What would now be considered an unusual arrest occurred on March 4, 1916 when 20 men were arrested for attending and betting on a cockfight that was being held on 11th Street hill. It has also been noted that the first city arrest of a drunken driver took place during October of 1923. In 1924, prisoners were brought to the station in a motorcycle sidecar.

The department continued to grow during the 1920s and 1930s with recognition throughout the county and the state that Beaver Falls had a police force second to none. The officers were tough, hard, and uncompromising, but they were also fair men who knew their duty and did it with pride.

As the 1920s drew to a close, the face of crime changed and so did the professional policemen's approach to coping with it. Although their word was still

POLICE DEPARTMENT, 1993. From left to right are the following: (front row) Jones, Guza, Reynolds, Burdine, Herst, and Miller; (middle row) Herman, Becze, Mazzant, Colbert, and Montani; and (back row) Straub, Alstadt, and Shotton.

law and their beat their own private domain, society had changed. Attitudes were different. Individuals had become more sophisticated, knowledgeable, and aware of their rights. Even though Beaver Falls was certainly no major crime center, city incidents now reflected the times. During the early years, a kid stealing fruit or bullying another child, or perhaps a domestic quarrel, a fight, or an encounter with a drunk, was an average day. But now the thefts were larger and they occurred more often. Robberies were committed and bootlegging was conducted and once in a while, gunfire could be heard. It called for a different type of policeman. Someone who was more alert and more intelligent, and the Beaver Falls force adjusted to the change and responded to the challenge.

One of the most famous and shocking crimes which horrified city residents took place on October 24, 1919 with the bank robbery and cold-blooded murder of a prominent citizen. His name was Vincent Sakraida, the bank director whose wife would later manage a highly successful women's dress store in the city for many years.

On that fateful day, two armed and brazen gunmen entered what was then the State Bank, located at 14th Street and Seventh Avenue. They ruthlessly murdered one victim and attempted to murder three other employees while robbing the bank of $9,000. It was close to closing time when the gunmen entered the building. Sakraida was writing out the final deposit while chatting with his brother John, who was also an employee. When the two men loudly announced a hold-up was in progress, the bank director quickly tossed the bonds into a wastebasket while his brother handed over the cash.

As the bandits ordered the safe opened, another employee, H.J. Peirsol, managed to press the alarm button alerting the police. As one of the gangsters grabbed the money on the counter, Vincent Sakraida gripped his hand, causing the surprised robber to shoot him in the head. Even while falling, Sakraida firmly kept his grip on the gunmen. Angered and frightened, the killer shot twice more, striking Sakraida in the breast and also hitting the floor. The brave Peirsol dove at the other bandit, tackling him around the knees. The thug shot at Peirsol three times, but missed on each occasion. John Sakraida was shot three times. He sustained a shoulder wound, a breast wound, and a grazed shot along his head. Defiantly, even though seriously wounded, he pursued the fleeing bandits outside and managed to toss a cuspidor at them before collapsing.

The panicky gunmen leaped into their vehicle, a Paige touring car, and sped north on Seventh Avenue. As they pulled away, they fired two more shots through the bank window, creating much fear and excitement to nearby people on the street, including local doctor J. Howard Swick, who immediately ran to the scene.

Beaver Falls police quickly gave chase under the command of Chief M.J. Coyne and the car was later found abandoned near Hookstown. A massive search was mounted and a $2,500 reward posted, but the men were never apprehended. Legend has it they were members of the Pretty Boy Floyd gang.

The times had certainly changed. Murder had reared its ugly head in Beaver Falls. Armed robbery, gambling, and even some small instances of prostitution were going on. The city was not a major crime area or a cesspool of sin, but equally so, it was not the innocent, uncomplicated city of only ten years before.

By this time, modern police techniques and a more sophisticated, scientific approach to police enforcement were being introduced and utilized across the nation by more progressive departments. Beaver Falls kept up with the times.

During the 1920s and 1930s, the force averaged 15 to 18 men. The Keystone Cop uniforms had long since departed and the men wore dark gray shirts with black trousers and heavy black winter coats. Patrol cars and motorcycles had replaced the horse although the beat patrolmen were still an important aspect of police work. Communications were much more developed with a full-time officer now working the desk, taking calls and relaying messages. Much more comprehensive files were being maintained and a better working relationship and communication with such agencies such as the state police and the FBI were established. Beaver Falls and its police force could no longer be isolated from the rest of society.

In 1933, Cora Blackledge was hired as the juvenile authority officer, a position she held for over a decade. A dedicated, no-nonsense woman who did her work to the letter of the law, she would earn a reputation for toughness that would be remembered and spoken of long after her death.

In 1931, an officer was rehired on the force who had first been hired in 1915. His name was Adam Smakosz and he became one of the legendary city officers. Hired as a young officer shortly after the turn of the century when cars were still a novelty, Smakosz soon resigned to join the U.S. Army during World War I. Following the war, after marrying and starting a family, Smakosz tried other work, but his heart longed to be in police work. It was his dream, his life long ambition; he never wanted to be anything but a good policeman.

When he returned in 1931, he became a beat patrolman, eventually becoming a lieutenant and finally working the desk shift towards the end of his career. During his many years of service, Smakosz saw every change in department procedure and city history, and was involved in most of the prominent cases that occurred. His reputation as a stern but fair man preceded him and he was well known and respected by everyone, included the youngsters in the city.

Although a private, retiring individual who never actively sought recognition, Smakosz served as president of the Fellowship of Police during 1947. His long career came to an end in 1963. Early in the year, as he worked traffic duty following a sports event, he was struck by an auto, which resulted in a broken hip. He was in a body cast until June and retired shortly thereafter ending a 32-year tenure.

In 1947, yet another local resident was hired who became a high-profile member of the police department. Ted Smith joined the force after having served with distinction as a military policeman with both the U.S. Marines and the U.S. Army. He worked his way up through the ranks as a patrolman and detective, and become chief in 1954 following the resignation of William Feeney. Smith would remain as chief until 1958 when he became a Beaver County detective.

FRANK POLICARO. Mr. Policaro was a police officer, a city police chief, and later Beaver County Sheriff.

Smith's big moment came on September 8, 1952 when he arrested Leonard Joseph "Bad Eye" Zalutsky, one of the FBI's 10 most wanted. Working on a tip and following some intensive investigation, Smith and fellow officer Gene Platt confronted the fugitive at his rented establishment in the lower part of Beaver Falls. After the arrest, Zalutsky attempted suicide, but was stopped by Smith and chief Bill Feeney. Smith received national media attention for the capture. He died in July of 1972.

The second Beaver Falls police officer to die on duty was Joe Galizia. Hired in 1945, Galizia perished in a car crash on June 9, 1953. Frank Policaro Jr. also achieved recognition through his police career. A city resident, Frank was hired as a member of the force in 1956 and rose to the rank of captain before retiring in 1976. At that time, he was elected sheriff of Beaver County, a position he still holds. Policaro was recently elected president of the National Sheriff Association.

The most beloved policeman in city history was "Big John" Jackson who was hired October 22, 1951. He was a giant of a man standing 6 feet 3 inches tall and

SARAH GRANT. Sarah was hired as a meter maid in 1977. She always has a smile for everyone and always helps anyone she can as she patrols the streets.

weighing 285 pounds. A former standout football player, Jackson was an imposing, even frightening sight as he patrolled the streets of Beaver Falls, and many an offender of the law would feel the unbelievable strength of his huge hands.

Fortunately for humanity, "Big John" was blessed with a gentle nature and a love for everyone. Unless proven otherwise, everyone was John's friend and his flashing smile, easy laugh, and big booming voice were known to every city resident. Respected and loved, he was adored by most of the children in the city unless they had committed an offense. They found that beneath the friendly, warm exterior was a determined policeman who would accept no foolishness. Jackson rose to the rank of captain before retiring in early 1978 to become a member of the Beaver County sheriff's department, where he served until the mid-1980s.

The years and events kept rolling by. The nature of crime changed with each new decade and police procedure had to be adjusted. The 1960s saw the first beginnings of the drug problem. Disobedience on the part of young people and disrespect for the law became commonplace until in the early 1980s, the size of the department climbed to a force of 23 men.

Parking meters had been installed March 20, 1947, and at first the police handled them until the duty was assumed by the parking authority. The first meter maids were Stella McGarry and June Kairis, hired on April 7, 1966.

The first policewoman in city history was Carolyn Crawford, who was hired in 1943. She was assigned to work the desk as a dispatcher. In 1950, Edith Smith and Clara Krall were hired as school crossing guards and in 1955, policemen began their first year working a 40-hour week. On June 17, 1975, Vivian Ruth Linta was hired as the first civilian dispatcher.

A police dog K-9 unit was introduced in 1971. The first officers assigned to work with their own dog were Don Burdine, Stan Guza, Paul Moore, "Skip" Haswell, and Wayne Rankin. Later officer Bob Jones would also be assigned to the unit. Although highly effective and praised by law enforcement agencies, the unit was eventually forced to disband when the city budget could no longer afford the price of upkeep. It is hoped that eventually the unit can be brought back into service.

In 1876, when Beaver Falls was only eight years in existence and had a population of about 3,000, the first volunteer fire department was organized. At that time, the volunteer company was handicapped by lack of equipment, but after the big conflagration at Graff Axe Works in March 1875, Henrici and Lenz of the Harmony Society solved the problem. They offered to build and equip an engine house if the borough would pay 6 percent interest on the investment. Borough council accepted the proposition and contracts were awarded.

In April 1875, the Silsby fire engine, hook-and-ladder wagon, and two hose carriages arrived and, with the rest of their "fixings," were paraded down Main Street to the Beaver Falls Cutlery where they were to be housed for a short time until the fire house was completed and everything was tested. Alexander Graham and Jim Perrott acted as nozzle men at the testing.

The "Steamer" was built by the Silsby Manufacturing Company of Seneca Falls, New York and was named "Jonathan Lenz" in honor of that distinguished gentleman. The hook-and-ladder wagon and hose carriages were built by S.M. Stewart of Rochester, New York.

It seems that in the very early days of the fire department, most of the male population of the borough were members. As nearly as can be determined at the time of organization, the equipment of the fire department consisted of a hand pump, a hose reel, a few leather buckets, and a couple of axes, and was housed on Fourth Street.

In 1875, when the firehouse on the northwest corner of 11th Street and Seventh Avenue was completed, fire equipment was moved to it from the Beaver

Falls Cutlery. The cost of the new firehouse was $8,900 and the new equipment cost around $8,000. It is interesting to note that in one history (written in 1903) the following statement is made:

> The engine house on the corner of 11th Street and Seventh Avenue, which has a commanding view of every portion of the town, was purchased in August 1890 for $25,000 and is now the property of the borough.

In 1881, the original volunteer fire company disbanded, but some of the larger property owners in Beaver Falls realized the need for a continued fire fighting organization. John Reeves, the venerable citizen and banker, as president, and Dr. William Raymer as secretary, headed this organization. The first fire chief in the Beaver Falls fire department was Mr. McComber in 1880.

There also is an interesting notation from one of the histories which states, "In 1875, when the steam engine arrived, the crowds swarmed about the engine and crawled on the seats, peered into the smoke stacks, rubbed their hands over the bright nickel plating and annoyed the engineer with remarks and suggestions. W.P. Allen and John Kerr were detailed as police to see that the curious were kept at a distance."

The first trained horses were purchased by the borough for the fire department in 1900. Prior to this, when the fire bell rang, the first team to arrive at the firehouse was pressed into service. It seems that $5 was paid to the owner of the first team to arrive and it was reported by one historian that when the bell rang, there were so many teams rushing to the firehouse that the dust from the dirt streets completely blacked out the town. There are tales of many narrow escapes the companies had from smashing themselves and their machines to pieces on the rocks, stumps, and ungraded streets.

On April 6, 1887, the fire company disbanded. It seems that the firemen and a number of the borough fathers did not see eye to eye on a number of issues, and all the property of the company was sold at auction. The event caused quite a stir, while the local and Pittsburgh papers were teeming with accounts of injustice done the department, which had done such a gallant service. During the next two years, repeated efforts were made to reorganize the company, but each failed. On April 4, 1880, council asked the old company to reorganize and it did. In 1895, the company was again disbanded, but it was reorganized the same year.

On July 14, 1887, there was a fire company know as "Beaver Falls Company No. 2" organized and located in what was then Barnard Town (now the north end of the downtown area). The station was located in the alley between 24th and 25th Streets and Ninth Avenue. The equipment consisted of a hand drawn hose reel with 500 feet of hose. When a fire call was sounded in the downtown area, the men would pull it to the streetcar line and wait for a streetcar to come along and hitch a ride, pulling the hose reel behind. The membership consisted of a few local prominent citizens.

In March of 1900, the borough hired the first full-time firemen. There were Charles Medley, chief, at a salary of $50 a month; and William Prudence, driver. On July 1, 1900, the borough purchased the first team of horses. This famous team was called "Billie and John" and they were used to draw the big engine for many years.

A statement taken from one history states the following:

> The horses added to the department make a vast difference in the running time. More hose, with hand fire extinguishers, smoke respirators and other appliances for fighting fires, places the company far ahead of any similar size towns for 100 miles around.

On June 1, 1900, a new hose wagon was built by S.M. Stewart Company of Rochester, New York and put into service. On April 1, 1908, a new combination chemical and hose wagon was put into service replacing the 1900 hose wagon.

Progress is necessary as time marches on, but is quite often sad. Such was the case when in 1917 the horse drawn engines became history. An entry was made in the fire log book which simply states: "Fire call, Rear Sixth Avenue; house—owner, Mrs. Copley—12:15 p.m. Horse John's last run." Checking the logbook today, one would find out that John made three runs that day. Fire calls are still logged in the same book today. A paragraph taken from a 1917 history stated:

ORNIE BIXLER. Mr. Bixler is driving John and Billy, the last horses used before motorizing the fire department, on 13th Street beside the library.

When two taps of the fire gong sound, "fire is out" for old John, the faithful horse and friend of the firemen, there will be many a sad heart around the City Building. Tears may be shed and the firemen will not be ashamed. For 17 long years, old John has answered the call. In storm and in sunshine, he has assisted his mates to draw the hose truck to many fires and never faltered. Old John has been burned; he has been cut by glass, struck by falling timbers, and gone lame, but in all his 17 years of service he has been out of commission for only 3 weeks. John is 21 years old and was purchased from Frank Dickey of East Liverpool, Ohio. A modern motor fire truck will soon replace him. Old John was retired to the Ira Duncan farm in Darlington on April 15, 1917. So closes forever a colorful chapter of history.

Through a quirk of good luck in 1962, the original apparatus that held the horse's harness was discovered at the old 11th Street station and donated to the fire department. If one were to visit the City Museum today, they would find this apparatus on display, as well as a number of other fire department relics from the past.

The harness was used in the days of the horse drawn steamers. The horses would be backed under this apparatus and by pulling a release, the harness would drop onto the horses, hooking them to the steamer. As the horses pulled the steamer out of the Fire House it would pass over a gas flame, which would ignite

CITY BUILDING. *Taken on August 16, 1934, the fire department shows off its new fire trucks. This building is located on 15th Street and Eighth Avenue.*

a fire in the firebox located under the steamer. As the horses raced to the fire scene, a draft was picked up by the air rushing into the firebox, causing it to ignite quickly. By the time the steamer reached the fire scene, the firebox had a raging fire within causing steam in the boiler, which in turn propelled the water pump within this piece of equipment. A small amount of coal was carried at the rear of the steamer to maintain the heat until arriving at the scene, where the neighbors in the area supplied additional fuel.

In 1917, the first motorized equipment was put into service. This consisted of a 1917 American-LaFrance chemical truck at a cost of $5,500 and a 1917 GMC hose truck at a cost of $2,300.

In 1927, construction was started on the building of the present fire station at 15th Street and Eighth Avenue. The fire department moved from the old station into the present one on September 13, 1928.

When the Borough of College Hill was incorporated into the city, College Hill Fire Department did not become Beaver Falls Company No. 2 until 1928. The history of this company goes back to March 1913. At the time of organization, there were 15 members in this department and the first fire chief was William Cain.

The first fire station on College Hill was located in the old Electric Power and Light building, which was located on 35th Street at the rear of the present fire station. The first fire truck on College Hill was purchased in 1914. It was a 1914 Nyeburg, 40-gallon chemical truck that cost $1,800.

Prior to 1920, there was only one fire hydrant located in the College Hill area. It was located at 32nd Street and Fourth Avenue and was owned by Geneva College. In 1920, 62 fire hydrants were installed in this area and 600 feet of fire hose was purchased by the borough. In 1922, Roy Davidson became fire chief and held this position until his retirement in 1963. In 1925, an American-LaFrance chemical truck replaced the Nyeberg chemical truck with two 40-gallon tanks at a cost of $8,750. In 1939, under a Public Works Administration grant, the present College Hill station (located on 35th Street and Sixth Avenue) was constructed at a cost of $34,000. On November 11, 1939, the company moved into the present building, which was dedicated on January 1, 1940.

In 1954, a volunteer association was organized by a group of citizens in the Pleasantview area of the city. Due to a number of problems, however, this organization was not recognized by the city until 1958, when it then became Beaver Falls Company No. 3. This company received its first truck in 1960 when a new pumper was put into service at the downtown station and the 1952 pumper from downtown was moved to the Pleasantview station, located in the 1600 block of 16th Avenue.

In 1963, the three fire companies were reorganized into one company. This reorganization was done to better consolidate training of the firemen and to make a more efficient and less complicated operation. This operation is used today. Although there are three districts, the downtown station, the College Hill station, and Pleasantview station, they operates as one company.

Here are some entries that were taken from the department's logbook:

1875 – Graff Axe Works [also two more times]
1879 – Howard Stove Company
1880 – Great Western File Workers
1880 – Baker Wagon Iron & Chain Works
1881 – Beaver Falls Steel Works
1881 – Mayer Pottery Company
1882 – Emerson Saw Works
Jan 15, 1886 – Beaver Falls Car Works
Dec 20, 1886 – Bradens Livery Stable
1887 – Pittsburgh Hinge Company
Nov 19, 1888 – Beaver Falls Iron Works
1889 – Cooperative Flint Glass
1892 – Whitla Glass Company
1894 – Carnegie Phipps Nail Mill
1895 – Turners Hall
Oct 21, 1896 – Mayer Pottery
1902 – Keystone Driller Company
Feb 12, 1905 – Penn Bridge Works
1910 – Union Drawn
1921 – Murphy Foundry Company
Jan 14, 1924 – G.C. Murphy Company – est. loss – $49,000
Mar 10, 1938 – G.C. Murphy Company – est. loss – $200,000
Oct 1, 1949 – City Market – est. loss – $50,000
July 2, 1952 – Powell Garage
Feb 16, 1956 – Metropolitan Bus Company
Dec 21, 1959 – A&P Supermarket – est. loss – $320,000
Apr 23, 1962 – Garvin Hardware – est. loss – $200,000
Jan 4, 1964 – F.W. Woolworth Co. & other stores – est. loss $430,000
Dec 22, 1965 – Berkmans – est. loss – $450,000
July 11, 1966 – E & B Casket Company – est. loss – $100,000
Nov 10, 1967 – Mason Bldg. – est. loss – $44,500
Apr 8, 1968 – Salvation Army – est. loss – $30,000
July 22, 1968 – R.E. Chambers – est. loss – $25,000
Jan 4, 1972 – Otterbein Methodist Church – est. loss – $25,000
Sept 12, 1972 – Thomas Industries (Ing-Rich) – est. loss – $50,000
Jan 17, 1973 – Record Shop – est. loss – $40,000
Mar 7, 1973 – Armstrong Cork – est. loss – $30,000
Oct 25, 1973 – Tusca Plastics – est. loss – $547,500
July 16, 1974 – Beaver Thermex – est. loss – $20,9000
Jan 11, 1975 – Sahli Building – est. loss – $40,000
May 8, 1976 – Apartment House – (1 fatality) – est. loss – $17,000
1980 – Dr. E.C. Dunn – est. loss – $117,000

R.C. GARVIN AND SONS, INC. Taken on April 23, 1962, the Garvin Hardware fire had an estimated loss over $200,000. The store was located in the 1700 block of Seventh Avenue.

1982 – Stanley Anderson Home – est. loss – $29,000
1983 – 2625 10th Avenue – (1 fatality) – est. loss – $6,000
Jan 14, 1993 – Incendiary (Arson) – est. loss – $5,000
Jan 20, 1992 – Republic Steel – est. loss – $7,000

As Beaver Falls continued to grow and prosper, it was evident that a decision had to be made in conjunction with health care. The welfare of the residents in this area was of growing concern to many of the city's civic and political leaders. Many meetings were held and long discussions ensued as to finding a solution for an obvious growing need.

Thus it was that in 1909, the Reverend J.M. Wertz, then pastor of Saint Mary's Catholic Church, authorized the purchase of the H.W. Reeves property, a 2-acre lot that contained a 14-room mansion. A few months later, four Sisters of Charity arrived from Seton Hill in Greensburg, Pennsylvania with all of $10 in their possession to begin what would become Providence Hospital.

It is difficult now to envision the almost insurmountable problems they encountered or the countless hours of extremely hard work and dedication they poured into their task. It was a time when the medical profession would be judged quite quaint, even primitive, by our modern day standards, but the sisters

H.W. REEVES HOME. Located on Third Avenue, it was purchased in 1909. The Sister's of Charity turned the 14-room mansion into the beginnings of Providence Hospital.

persisted and were determined to make their hospital one of the most up to date facilities in the country.

It was on October 13, 1909 that the very first patient was admitted for treatment and was attended by Dr. J.F. Jackson. Later in the day, the second patient was admitted and attended by Dr. J. Howard Swick. The doctors carried patients back to their beds after surgery since there was not enough staff available. The original structure when it opened had only 22 available beds. It was quickly apparent that the facility would have to expand to keep up with the enormous health needs of the rapidly growing city. More and more sisters were added to the staff and more trained nurses were hired.

The first annex was soon added in 1912 and a training school for nurses established. Each year, more improvements were made, including fresh paint, new flooring, the addition of much needed rooms, and of course the purchase and acquisition of the newest, most modern equipment.

In 1923, five young ladies graduated from the nursing school and the Terrazzo floors were installed in the men's ward and also in the second and third floor corridors. But even with all the new improvements and better-trained staff, hospital costs still averaged only $3 a day. This included meals and special care.

During 1931, 1,032 patients were treated at the facility with the average patient staying about two weeks. As many as 575 operations were performed and 152 births recorded. By 1932, the records showed that over 19,000 patients had been treated. Of the total, approximately 25 percent were free patients and 10 percent were part-pay patients. About 1,600 babies had been delivered over the years and it was plain to see that the hospital was a vital, contributing factor to the success of the city.

In 1938, a grant provided money for the building of an up-to-date expansive laboratory and X-ray department. In 1939, the adjacent Marcus property was acquired and in 1940, the Roman property was purchased and utilized the following year as the nurses' quarters.

In 1945, another annex to the hospital was dedicated. The cornerstone-laying ceremony took place on Sunday, March 25 at 2:30 p.m. at the hospital. Many dignitaries were present and a large crowd was on hand. Judge Robert E. McCreary was the guest speaker and the Beaver Falls High School Band, under the direction of A.J. Pletinicks, provided music.

Continuing to grow and becoming ever more complex over the years, Seton Hall, a new nurses' residence, was built in 1952 and two new wings added to the hospital in 1958 as a result of a $1.35-million expansion program.

An important step was taken in 1965 when the Providence and New Brighton of Beaver Valley General were combined. Mr. Luke E. Sawyer was elected head of the united hospital board and Milton Appleyard became executive director of both units, which were run separately.

Up to this point, there had been numerous personalities and outstanding staff administrators who had made considerable impact within the community and had

SISTER M. IRENAEUS. The Sister is a living legend in Beaver Valley nursing and was Pennsylvania's outstanding nurse of the year in 1966. Being the administrator of Providence Hospital from 1924 to 1959, she was a true Sister of Charity.

become well-known figures. Sister M. Irenaeus was hospital administrator and superior of the Sisters of Charity from 1924 to 1959 and headed the school of nursing from 1914 to 1917. The nursing school began in 1912 and graduated its first five nurses in 1915. Sister Irenaeus was also recognized at state levels as an outstanding nurse and was probably the most admired and loved sister ever to serve the hospital.

In 1946, she was made a fellow of the American College of Hospital Administrators, one of the highest honors that could be bestowed upon her. She was known for her love and dedication to the caring and welfare of the patients and stressed working together for the good of the hospital with all religions. She was also known for her famous walks along the business district and in various stores just to meet and greet people. Due to the stress and pressure of her job, she found it a pleasant way of relaxing. Sister Irenaeus passed away on October 16, 1976 at the age of 103.

Another well-known sister was Sister Mary Kieran, who was the medical and surgical supervisor before replacing Sister Irenaeus as administrator in 1959.

Two city ladies strongly identified with the hospital were Miss Bessie A. Hanley and Ann Mutschellar whose combined services to the facility in the administrative capacity totaled 92 years.

By 1963, Providence had grown to 137-bed capacity in addition to 19 bassinets. The hospital had grown to 220 employees, including 70 registered nurses, with an annual budget of $1.2 million. However, changes were taking place that were seriously affecting the hospital. Society itself was changing and a more advanced technology and medical advances demanded a more modern and sophisticated business approach to maintaining such a complex establishment. It became more and more apparent that the sisters were no longer capable of keeping up with the increasing daily problems.

Finally on March 1, 1967, what had once been considered unthinkable happened when the Sisters of Charity left the hospital after six decades of dedicated service. Close to 400 sad people attended a community testimonial at the Hotel Broadhead and the sisters were presented a certificate of merit from the Beaver Falls Area Chamber of Commerce and a distinguished service award from the Upper Beaver Valley Jaycees. It marked the end of an era and signaled a forbidding future.

Shortly after the sisters' departure, the hospital instituted 24-hour emergency care amid growing rumors that plans were underway for the construction of a huge new hospital complex that would make most area hospitals obsolete.

Throughout the late 1960s, the rumors persisted that the days of the hospital were numbered. The new trend across the nation was merger; merger of companies, businesses, sports complexes, small communities and yes, hospitals. The hospital kept up its high standards and continued to add modern equipment and maintain its staff, but it grew more obvious that the handwriting was on the wall.

Finally in late 1970, it was announced that the Beaver County Joint Hospital Planning Association that had been formed in 1968 would build a huge medical complex after a long study.

PROVIDENCE HOSPITAL. L.G. Kirker and Company contractors added the first annex to the hospital in 1912. The building is located on Third Avenue.

This created a huge public outcry of opposition, which featured angry protests in local newspapers, editorials, radio talk shows, and town meetings. A hospital is a vital, integral part of a city, a symbol, and a reassuring presence that harbors a lifetime of family memories. But opposition or not, it was evident that changing times, attitudes, and social conditions made the decision to build a new complex inevitable.

In July of 1971, Mr. And Mrs. Michael Baker Jr. offered to generously donate 100 acres of land in Brighton Township for a construction site. The offer was accepted and negotiated upon and finally on June 6, 1977, after years of studies, threatened lawsuits, and bitter controversy, groundbreaking ceremonies were held and construction of the new 500-bed facility began. The project eventually cost $54.5 million.

Little by little, piece by piece, the Providence Hospital was slowly dismantled. On June 3, 1980, the last surgery was performed and on June 5 and 6, the last pieces of equipment were moved out. On Friday, June 6, the emergency unit closed its doors forever. A profound sense of loss and sadness covered the city.

For a short period of time, the edifice stood silent and empty. The wind rattled unwashed windows; dry leaves gathered in mounds upon un-walked sidewalks and the ghosts of many well known, respected physicians surely walked the empty corridors at night. There were many beloved doctors, colorful, dedicated personalities who were deeply associated with the hospital history. A mere handful of the best, when remembered, bring back warm memories.

The first physician to venture as far west as Beaver Valley was Dr. Samuel Adams, who came from Massachusetts before 1800, bought 400 acres of land (comprising what is now the territory lying between 17th and 26th streets, the Beaver River, and Mt. Washington). With the exception of Dr. Adams and his son Dr. Milo Adams, most of the early doctors following the wagon trails west stopped where the wagons stopped—namely, in Darlington, Hookstown, and Greensburg—rather than in the Beaver Falls area.

Early physicians ranged from ones extremely active in community affairs to ones positively opposed to any community participation, believing that they best served their community by giving full attention to professional labors.

Dr. W.R. Raymer, who came to Beaver Falls in 1878, was at various times a burgess, commissioner's clerk of the county, and treasurer of Beaver Falls Building & Loan, while Dr. A.S. Moon (son of Dr. R.A. Moon) refused to participate in any community affairs.

The image which so many have of the "horse and buggy" doctor is indeed more truth than fiction. Dr. J.S. Louthan, for instance, practiced just that way and patients signed their names on a slate in his office for house calls to be made as

J. HOWARD SWICK SR. Dr. Swick and his son Emerson are shown in his new Maxwell, which was purchased at the B.O. Fair Garage. Emerson died in childhood. This picture was taken on Seventh Avenue and 18th Street.

time permitted. Dr. Samuel Adams would be gone for days at a time, and his wife became proficient in dispensing medicines and even in setting fractures.

Some Beaver Falls physicians came to medicine through other fields. Dr. J.D. McCarter was a schoolteacher before starting his medical practice in 1883. Incidentally, Dr. McCarter's great grandmother was reported to be the first white woman to cross the Ohio River at Beaver. Dr. John C. Gaston was first an engineer.

Dr. T.G. McPherson, the first doctor in Patterson Township (which in 1866 had about 100 inhabitants), was an accomplished writer. After practicing for 36 years, he devoted his retirement years to his literary pursuits. Dr. H.S. McGoun was first a pharmacist and later a commercial traveler, and had the distinction of being a member of the victorious army at the close of the Civil War.

Dr. J. Howard Swick was both a physician and a highly effective, respected U.S. Congressman. The good doctor began practicing in the city on October 1, 1906. Serving as a doctor during World War I, he was discharged with the rank of major and retaining his commission, he rose to the permanent rank of colonel. He was a city councilman from 1922 until 1926, when he was elected to Congress. He was re-elected three times, serving a total of eight years. Not only was he a respected physician and politician, Dr. Swick was also active in numerous civic groups, clubs, commissions, and boards until his death on November 17, 1952.

Perhaps the most beloved doctor in city history was Dr. Cedric Dunn. A hometown boy, local high school graduate, and Geneva College student, Ced, as he was called, also worked at numerous local businesses to earn his way through college and medical school. He graduated in 1936 with honors and was president of his class at Hahnemann Medical College in Philadelphia. He was 19 years of age.

Returning to Beaver Falls, "Doc" Dunn took over the old Dr. Simpson office on 13th Street, which still used gaslights and featured a log-burning fireplace in the waiting room. This was a different time and age, and it was nothing for him to put in a long office day and then make house calls until long after midnight. Most medicine was distributed at the office and a large percentage of babies were delivered at home. Many of us still fondly recall being given the sugar candy pills in a small capsule with a cork top at the conclusion of a visit.

Dunn became known as the baby doctor, having delivered more than 14,000 throughout the area during his many years of practice. His first delivery was rather remarkable when he was flagged down by police officer Adam Smakosz, for what he thought to be an appendicitis attack turned out to be a baby. The highly popular doctor continued to serve his patients, although towards the end on a much more limited basis until the mid-1970s. Dr. Dunn is enjoying a well-deserved retirement at his home on College Hill in Beaver Falls.

R. Kevin Carugati, M.D. is a graduate of Beaver Falls High School. He was raised on College Hill and attended Saint Philomena Church. He is the son of the late Richard I. Carugati and Roseanelle Price Carugati. Kevin is married to Jane Carugati and has two daughters, Kati and Christine. Dr. Carugati and his wife take an active role in civic and humanitarian as well as religious roles in the community. He purchased the former Dr. Ronald Kludo practice located at 10th Street and Eighth Avenue. His office is located in the former home of Meryl Moltrup, one of the early aviation pioneers. Dr. Carugati practices the one-on-one type of medicine practiced by our pioneer physicians of Beaver County. Such is the quality and caliber of only a few of the outstanding city physicians.

The hospital was much too large a building, with enormous potential, to be left to decay and become a slum. Many people determined that its contribution to the city was far from over. One of those people was local proprietor Maurice Mervis, who for many years had been the owner and manager of Hoffman's Drug Store and a city property owner. Mervis felt the loss of the hospital was a disgrace along with being an economic blow to the city that was devastating. The waste of such a building was, in his opinion, an outrage and he decided to do something about it.

First, Mervis negotiated with the Medical Center of Beaver County to purchase it. Then he had to seek permission from the Federal Health Systems Agency to renovate it into a 179-bed nursing home. He then sought the aid of the County Industrial Development Authority to provide him with more than $2 million in low interest financing to cover the cost. Then he had to gain the approval of the Beaver County Commissioners.

Finally, all the steps were taken and approvals given and by April of 1981, Mervis announced the former hospital would reopen by late August as the Providence Health Care Center, Inc. of Beaver Falls, containing 180 beds while giving extended and intermediate medical care.

"We selected the name, Providence, because it means and represents so much to city residents," Mervis stated. "We will be self operating and provide all of our own services.

The Health Care Center did indeed open early in 1982 and has continued to operate successfully to this day. A positive sign that the facility that began so many years before, through the prayers, determination, and dedication of the Sisters of Charity, will continue to be a vital contributing factor in the progress and history of Beaver Falls.

3. Place of Many Faiths

What was it that brought people to settle on a 3-mile stretch of the Beaver River, first in a gathering called Brighton, then Old Brighton, and then from November 9, 1868 onward in the town incorporated as Beaver Falls, Pennsylvania? This is where the jobs were, and so came men and women of many nationalities; and they built the industrial plants, roads, bridges, and other elements of infrastructure that humans require in Western civilization. The early settlers were English, Scotch, and Irish. The Economites were of German ancestry. They imported Chinese for the local cutlery. At the turn of the century came the influx of other nationalities: middle Europeans, Italians, and African Americans coming from the south and deep south seeking a better way of life and employment. They are the ones who helped build the railroads, the bridges, the roads, the streets and sewers, the streetcar lines, the buildings and housing, and provided labor for the burgeoning industrial plants and transportation systems of the late nineteenth and early twentieth centuries.

One early settler, Dr. Adams and his family, were members of the Methodist faith and held meetings in their log cabin home. Dr. Adams was also a minister of the Methodist Church. Another early settler, John White, was a very devout Covenanter who was a member of the Reformed Presbyterian Church. Many believe that the Little Red Schoolhouse is where Quaker meetings were held, as many of the early families were Quakers. The Patterson family had members put in crypts under the old Saint Mary's Episcopal Church while the Reeves family was active in several churches in town. After the Harmony Society bought Patterson's property at sheriff sale in 1859, a large influx of Germans brought the Lutheran and Roman Catholic faiths into the area. With the building of the Erie Canal came the Irish and Scotch-Irish bringing both Presbyterian and Roman Catholic faiths. Around the time of the Civil War, members of the Jewish faith settled in the Beaver Valley. From this mixture of nationalities grew the 38 different churches located within the city limits of Beaver Falls. The author wishes to apologize in advance if anyone feels slighted because his or her particular place of worship is not mentioned in the following narrative. The amount of information that could be put into this book was limited.

SAINT PAUL'S EVANGELICAL LUTHERAN CHURCH. The church was founded in 1926 and was located at 501 37th Street on College Hill. The present building was dedicated in 1958.

The spiritual life of a community reflects strongly upon the personality of its residents and the city itself. Throughout the long history of Beaver Falls, religion has traditionally played a very important role. For quite a long period of time, both church leaders and layman were instrumental in forming policy, creating business, and guiding government in decisions affecting future growth and progress.

After the entire borough had been purchased and owned by the very strict Harmony Society, their rules and attitude dominated many aspects of the early settlers. Much later, Saint Mary's Roman Catholic Church purchased large tracts of land and was eventually responsible for the foundation of Old Providence Hospital.

Many church affiliations had their origins in initial services in the Little Red Schoolhouse before being able to form their own church. The early Lutheran and Methodist churches all began this way.

Over the years, many outstanding laymen and members of the Presbyterian, Methodist, Lutheran, and Catholic churches have served in official city capacities, city government, or on commissions and authorities. The closely related ties between church and city seem very deep in Beaver Falls.

At one point in time, the city counted 38 active churches in residence. At this time, 32 churches are located within city boundaries. The input to the city by our religious community cannot be underestimated.

Early in 1883, 34 Baptists living in Beaver Falls met in the Little Red Schoolhouse and organized the Baptist Church in Beaver Falls. In 1884, the committee purchased two lots on what is now the corner of Sixth Avenue and 17th Street. During 1885, a red brick church was built and they received their charter and certificate of incorporation. In 1886, a mission was started as a Sunday school in the Mt. Washington area. During the same year, a plot of ground at 10th Avenue and 24th Street was deeded to the church. In 1888, the name "first" was added. By 1907, membership had grown and a new building was needed. The old church was razed and church services were held at the 24th Street Chapel. The new church was erected at the corner of Sixth Avenue and 17th Street. In 1966, plans were drawn up for further expansion.

The Second Baptist Church was organized under the leadership of Reverend G.D. Brown in 1894. The group met in the church building owned by First Baptist located at 10th Avenue and 24th Street (the present site of K&M Automotive Electric Service). The congregation grew and was soon able to build a church on a lot across 24th Street from the building owned by the First Baptist Church. In 1927, under Reverend G.F. Sallie Sr., the congregation began a massive building campaign. A spacious parsonage was built and the present church was begun. After a few years of tireless work, the building was completed. The Ingram-Richardson Company is given credit for helping the congregation pay off its debt.

The Tabernacle Baptist was given its start in 1919 under the leadership of Reverend Samuel Bush. During Reverend Bush's pastorate, a site at 610 Third Avenue was purchased. During Reverend S.M. Hall's pastorate (1924–1929), a

SECOND BAPTIST CHURCH. Located on Tenth Avenue and 24th Street, this church recently had a historical marker placed in front of it by the local landmark foundation.

church structure was built. The congregation later moved to 630 Third Avenue and built a new church. The current pastor is Reverend Calvin C. Brown, who has become one of the city's best-known and most beloved and respected personalities. He recently celebrated his 40th anniversary as a minister.

Downtown Beaver Falls once had three Roman Catholic churches, two of which were outgrowths of Saint Mary of the Immaculate Conception Church, dedicated July 4, 1872. Catholics from Beaver Falls had been attending Saint Joseph's Church across the river in New Brighton and, as early as 1868, started efforts to found a church of their own. They purchased two lots facing Sixth Avenue from the Harmony Society for $600. In 1871, a building was completed. In the 1890s, property off Darlington Road known as the old Saint Mary's Cemetery was purchased. In 1900, Father Wertz decided that Beaver Falls needed a hospital and in 1909, the hospital officially opened. In 1923, plans for the new school started and in 1935, the Tamaqua Club located across from the church on 10th Street was purchased and converted into a home for sisters teaching at the school. In 1944, it became necessary to expand the cemetery and the Grimm Farm was purchased along Darlington Road. Holy Trinity Catholic parish got its start in 1910 when 100 families of Polish descent indicated a desire for a separate church. In 1910, the former Lutheran church at the corner of 10th Street and Sixth Avenue was purchased. Holy Trinity would also have its own school where the Bernadine Sisters taught from 1917 until 1954. The Felician Sisters taught there

SAINT MARY'S ROMAN CATHOLIC CHURCH. *The building is located on Sixth Avenue and Tenth Street. Prior to 1896, the old church, which was built in 1871, is located near the site of Divine Mercy Academy.*

SAINT MARY'S STUDENTS. These students are from an early class at the turn of the century, c. 1900. Some of these students would become members of prominent Catholic families.

from 1955 to 1957 and the Sisters of Divine Providence taught there until 1959 when the teaching Order of Saint Joseph from Baden joined them. The school closed in 1969. The other downtown Catholic church was Saint Ladislaus, which was founded by families of Hungarian descent. In 1923, a church group was organized and the first mass was held at the old Polish church located on the corner of Sixth Avenue and 10th Street. Approximately 100 persons attended the mass. In 1924, the congregation purchased the brick church at the corner of Seventh Avenue and Ninth Street owned by the First Reformed Presbyterian congregation, which was moving to a new place of worship on Darlington Road. The church building was sold in 1985 and merged with Saint Mary's to become Divine Mercy in 1993. It is hard to believe that at one time Beaver Falls had three Catholic churches all located less than a block from each other.

By a decree issued by the Most Revered Hugh C. Boyle, bishop of Pittsburgh, the parish of Saint Philomena Catholic was established on College Hill. The present building was erected on ground purchased at Fourth Avenue and 40th Street. Since its founding, more than 1,000 persons have been baptized at Saint Philomena's. At the time of this writing, there are two Catholic schools offering a Christian education to students, Saint Phenomena's and Divine Mercy Academy.

Beaver County and the Upper Beaver Valley have a long history of members of the Jewish community living in the area. The first Hebrew congregation was

BEAVER VALLEY JEWISH COMMUNITY CENTER. Dedicated in 1959, the center was sold in the 1990s and the congregation moved to smaller quarters at 2634 Darlington Road in Chippewa. The building is now the Dialysis Clinic, Inc.

organized at New Brighton in April 1864 and moved to Beaver Falls about 1879. Since there was no regular rabbi, services were conducted by members and held in homes until 1904 when a charter for Agudas Achim Congregation was granted. In 1914, the synagogue on the corner of Fifth Street and Sixth Avenue was built and dedicated. In 1959, the Jewish Community Center was dedicated in Chippewa; it house two congregations, the conservative and the reform Beth Shalom. It provided complete religious, cultural, social, educational, and philanthropic programs. Due to a declining membership, the Community Center was sold in the 1990s and the congregation moved to smaller quarters. It is currently under the leadership of Rabbi Myer Asper. Many outstanding leaders of the community, including teachers and merchants, have been members of the Jewish faith. Beaver Falls would not be the great city that it is today had it not been for the Jewish influence.

In the city limits, Beaver Falls had six Methodist churches. The Methodist church goes back to the early 1800s and Dr. Adams. The First United Methodist Church got its start in the Little Red Schoolhouse. The first church building was built in 1868 and had been added to and remodeled over the years. The College Hill Methodist Church was established in 1907. The Central United Methodist Church started in the Little Red Schoolhouse in 1869. The first building was located at Third Avenue between Pine and Short Tenth Street where the Magyar (Hungarian) Presbyterian Church is currently located. In 1902, they moved to

13th Street and Sixth Avenue. The Primitive Methodist Church was organized in 1954 and in 1961 moved to its new church building located at the corner of Wallace Run and Shenango Roads. The Otterbein United Methodist Church was founded in 1901 at the corner of 19th Street and Seventh Avenue. It was originally called First Evangelical United Brethren Church. In 1946, the Evangelical Church and United Brethren in Christ merged into one. Later, they merged with the Methodist Church in 1968. The Riverview United Methodist Church located at the top of 11th Street Hill was founded in 1919 and was another Evangelical Church, which later joined the Methodist Church.

First Congregational was founded in 1888 and the church was built on Fourth Avenue. First Christian was organized in 1887 at the Little Red Schoolhouse. They built their church at the corner of 14th Street and Sixth Avenue. The present church was built in 1906.

The Salvation Army came to Beaver Falls in 1884. The Citadel on Seventh Avenue was gutted by fire in 1968. In 1973, the Fifth Avenue School closed and was sold to the Salvation Army. The site was razed and the new Citadel was erected.

First Methodist Episcopal Church. Located on Eighth Avenue and Tenth Street, it was built in 1868 and is now called the First Methodist Church.

Beaver Falls had nine Presbyterian churches at one time. Calvary United Presbyterian Church on 11th Street and Sixth Avenue was organized in 1869. In 1910, the mother church, Calvary United, organized the College Hill and Steffin Hill churches and in 1957 the Chippewa Presbyterian Church was formed.

Campbell United Presbyterian Church was formed in 1917. The church building is now the home of the Episcopal congregation of Christ, the King Episcopal Church. Geneva Reformed Presbyterian Church got its start in 1892. College Hill Reformed Church was formed in 1896 when 40 members of the Geneva church met to express their dissatisfaction with the policy—though not the doctrine—of the parent church. Immigrants from Hungary and Transylvania founded Third Avenue United Presbyterian Church in 1910. Trinity United Presbyterian started in the Little Red Schoolhouse in 1867. First Reformed Church was organized in 1874. They built a church at the corner of Ninth Street and Seventh Avenue in 1892. Fifty-eight members of the congregation took their certificates and organized the Geneva congregation on College Hill. In 1924, they sold the church building to the Saint Ladislaus Roman Catholic Church and moved to the new church located on Darlington Road in Patterson Township. Saint Mary's Episcopal was one of seven Episcopal Churches in Beaver County and was organized in 1870. They used to meet in the Little Red Schoolhouse. Their church would be built at the corner of Church Street and Eighth Avenue (Lincoln Place). In 1926, a stone from Westminster Abbey was placed in the church. Due to a decreasing attendance and shift in population, the church building was sold in 1991 to Weidner Engineering. The congregation later purchased the former Campbell Memorial Presbyterian Church building on College Hill and is now called Christ the King Episcopal Church.

Christian & Missionary Alliance Church was organized about 1904. In 1912, property at the corner of Eighth Avenue and 14th Street was purchased and a church was built. Later in the 1970s, a new church building was erected at 3629 37th Street Extension. The building at Eighth Avenue was sold and is now the home of Valley Baptist Church.

First Assembly of God organized in 1920 and combined with the First Romanian Pentecostal Church in 1959. In 1965, they purchased a 3-acre lot at 1300 Darlington Road and have since built a new church. The old church at the site of 25th Street and 10th Avenue is now the home of the Supreme Council of the House of Jacob.

Elder Thomas Griswald and the late Elder C.T. Toombs began Christ Temple Church of God in Christ in 1925. In 1960, the current church building at 2420 Ninth Avenue was erected. Elder Griswald would leave several sons who would become active members in the church and take an active part in community affairs.

College Hill Church of the Nazarene started as a tent meeting after World War II. They purchased property at 36th Street and Fourth Avenue and erected a very nice building.

For most of Beaver Falls's history, members of the Orthodox faith did not have a church in this part of the valley. The Orthodox churches were located in Midland, Aliquippa, or Ambridge. Therefore, members of the Orthodox faith had quite a distance to travel to attend services. In the late 1980s, an Orthodox church was added to the town's rich religious history at 15th Street and Eighth Avenue and was called Saint John's The Evangelist Orthodox Church.

To add to the list, there is also the Church of God in Mt. Washington, Community Temple Baptist, Faith Temple, United Pentecostal, Mayfield Bible Baptist Church, Cross & Crown Christian Fellowship, The House of The Lord Church, Jehovah's Witness Kingdom Hall, Beaver Valley Christian Fellowship, and Holy Spirit Fellowship Church.

FIRST UNITED PRESBYTERIAN CHURCH. This church was organized in 1869 and is located on 11th Street and Sixth Avenue. The present church was built under the pastorate of Dr. Robert W. Kidd in the 1890s and is now called Calvary United Presbyterian Church.

4. Entertainment and Leisure Time

As this book is being written, there are no longer any movie theaters located in the city of Beaver Falls. There have not been any since 1981 when a disastrous fire destroyed the last remaining structure. They're gone now, vanished through the mists of time and memory . . . all of the great classic city movie theaters. During the mid-century they were the meccas of local entertainment and every city or town had a least one.

During the golden age of movies, the 1930s through the 1950s, Beaver Falls had four movie theaters. They were huge, beautiful establishments that teasingly held out the promise of exciting, secret delights in their hidden, dark interiors. They introduced us to an unending variety of dreams, heroes, adventure, horror, and fantasy and beckoned us to unleash the chained limits of our imaginations to the fullest extent.

These lovely ornate buildings of culture and taste covered with rich decorations were the last stylish remnants of what is now a glorious but gone golden age.

Nearby Rochester had two theaters, the Family and the Oriental, while Beaver and New Brighton each had one. There were eight daily movie houses operating within a 3-mile radius.

But it was Beaver Falls, the giant entertainment center, that offered four theaters during the 1920s, 1930s, 1940s, and into the 1950s. This was the heyday of the film industry long before the advent of television, when the movie feature was king.

But, as it is with all things, change is constant. Radio began to dominate home entertainment and then came television. After World War II, people's attitudes changed, becoming more sophisticated and critical. New sources of entertainment and a better appreciation of live theater became accepted.

Because of these numerous changes in cultures and society, the age of the movie as the major source of entertainment quietly passed away and eventually, one by one, the local cinema houses began to stand silent gathering dust. Echoing sounds of laughter and applause had long since died away. Today's city youngsters are growing up with no conception or realization of the rich heritage in entertainment that Beaver Falls once had. Our four local theaters not only did good business, but they thrived, pulling in customers from all around the area.

RIALTO THEATER. This photo was taken shortly before the building was razed in the late 1960s. It was located on Seventh Avenue and Fifth Street.

Today, the Rialto and State Theaters have been torn down, the ground leveled for new business and the distant memories of those two showcases rapidly fading. The beautiful Granada is now a senior citizen center and the grand, glorious Regent stood desolate, a fire-gutted shell for a number of years, until it was razed and replaced by a medical complex. It's a sad, dismal end for four homes of magic enchantment.

The smallest and least attended of the four locals was the State Theater at 500 Seventh Avenue. Built by Hanauer Enterprises, it was originally called the Savoy and it opened to the public on November 7, 1907. Two-reel movies were shown along with vaudeville presentations in 1910. It was a relatively small building possessing only one floor and it presented both vaudeville and stage shows. Sam Hanauer was the manager. The structure was demolished in 1930 to create a parking lot for the nearby Rialto Theater. But in 1936, Hanauer Enterprises erected another new establishment. It was christened the State Theater and featured sound movies and reruns. It had no affiliated contract with any of the major movie studios.

Therefore, the State picked up the many smaller independent productions and less publicized films. Movies no one else wanted, quickie documentaries, cheap western and war films, and occasional European art films were shown. But many a small child was thrilled in the darkness because of the wild animal adventure

LYCEUM AND SAVOY THEATER. *Asher Hanauer built the Lyceum Theater in 1902 at 500 Seventh Avenue. The Savoy opened in 1907 and the name was changed to Rialto in 1928. The building was razed in 1930.*

documentary films of Martin and Oss Johnson featuring African big game or the exotic exploits of the famous Frank (Bring Em Back Alive) Buck and the highly popular films of his career capturing ferocious wild animals. He was later proven to be pretty much a phony, but at one time, Buck was one of America's greatest heroes.

The State may have been a small theater, but it looms large in many childhood memories. The State Theater closed forever in 1951. Located only a few doors down from the State was the beautiful, immaculate Rialto Theater, which possessed the prestigious, exclusive MGM distribution contract, thus giving the owners the rights to the leading studio quality films in the industry.

The edifice was originally named the Lyceum, which opened on December 2, 1902 and was again a property of Hanauer Enterprises. The showplace was located in what was then the center of town.

The glittering opening performance, which attracted a large and well-dressed audience, was *Rices Show Girl*, with the local Joseph Hardy Orchestra providing the music. The gala event was considered quite a social event and prominent Judge J. Sharp Wilson made some opening remarks. A subscription list for those wishing to sit in the boxes had been in circulation for some time. All boxes and the best single seats sold for $50 each, which was an enormous amount of money for that time. The remaining orchestra seats were priced at $1.50 each and every seat in the house was sold.

Dramas and musical comedies were offered to the public and many important productions were staged. Beaver Falls and the Lyceum played host to such outstanding performers as Charley Grapewin in the hit comedy *Awakening of Mr. Pipp*; Mrs. Fiske in *Ghosts*; DeWolf Hopper, known for his recitation of *Casey At the Bat*, appeared in *Wang*; and even the notorious Eva Tanguay, the scandalous "I Don't Care Girl" of Broadway, graced the floorboards.

In 1925, Ben Walken leased the theater and continued to book popular stage and burlesque shows, but he also added the exciting attraction of action movies. When his lease expired in 1927, the theater was temporarily closed. It was remodeled and opened again on October 22, 1928 as the Rialto. It still presented an occasional stage production, but mainly featured the top silent films of the day. By the early 1930s, sound equipment was installed and assured full attendance for its 900-seat capacity. The first talking feature was *Shady Lady* starring Phillis Haver.

Perhaps the most fondly remembered stage production was the local presentation of *Elks Minstrels* which ran for a number of years ending in 1935. In 1951, the Rialto hosted the "Miss Beaver Valley" contest.

Since the Rialto was the only theater that had the MGM contract, it gained the reputation of having the best quality films available. Only at that location could local audiences thrill to the adventures of Clark Gable, Spencer Tracy, and Joan Crawford, the majesty and spectacle of Quo Vadis, Ben Kelly, Jeanette MacDonald, and Nelson Eddy, or admire the beauty of Elizabeth Taylor. The Rialto stood for class, but it too fell upon dwindling attendance and hard times and was forced to close its doors forever. The once proud Rialto dimmed its lights for the final time in 1968.

In 1911, there was great excitement and anticipation as a huge new theater was opened at 1123 Seventh Avenue. William E. White, a local resident, had leased the property. The finished product, called the Colonial, had a 300-seat capacity.

Silent features were at their peak and local audiences thrilled to epic stories featuring such stars as Valentino, Garbo, the Barrymores, William S. Hart, King Baggot, Harold Lloyd, Buster Keaton, Ruth Chattertom, Clara Kimball Young, and Mary Miles Minter. Also packing in local film-goers were the highly popular Mack Sennett comedies featuring such great favorites as Ben Turpin, Chester Conklin, Mabel Norman, Charlie Chaplin, and of course the always popular Keystone Cops.

The theater closed for a short time in 1917 and reopened that same year as the New Colonial under the management of Mrs. Howard Dawson. In 1928, S. Goodman of Pittsburgh purchased the theater and completely remodeled it into the well-remembered exotic Spanish-type front with a large lighted marquee that extended well over the sidewalk. A huge city contest was conducted at this time to choose a new name for the attractive establishment and since it possessed a Spanish motif, the winning entry was the Granada.

The Granada was later acquired by Fred Cook of the Cook-Anderson Company in Beaver and was retained by them until its final closing on November 30, 1960. The Granada had contracts with RKO, Warner Brothers, Paramount, and Twentieth Century Fox, which allowed the customers a wide variety of films and stars to choose from. On any given week, patrons could watch Allan Ladd or Errol Flynn in a rousing western. Jane Russell, Betty Grable, Bette Davis, Veronica Lake, and Barbara Stanwyck were among the beauties on the screen. Gangster films crackled with the presence of immortals such as Cagney, Bogart, and Edward G. Robinson, while Doris Day and Gordon McCrea musicals left viewers humming.

The Granada, with its Spanish knights, tiered balcony, and overhead ceiling with airplanes and stars painted upon it, was a cherished treasured. But without question, the most beloved and popular theater in the city was the Regent. It was the number one cowboy movie-house for a decade. First known as the Alhambra, the building was constructed by local businessman John Paff in 1912. It was located at 1308 Seventh Avenue and opened in 1913. The building was an immense auditorium that had a main floor and two balconies. It boasted a 1,150-seat capacity.

The stage area and orchestra pit were the largest between Pittsburgh and Cleveland. Over the years, it would host country and western acts, magicians, lecturers, musicals and stage dramas, dance groups, and wrestlers. At one time, the Keith-Albee vaudeville circuit toured there and during 1915, the William T. Leuis Stock Company played for a season. Local talent programs were also produced in the imposing structure.

Western Pennsylvania Amusement Company of Pittsburgh obtained the theater in 1918. The huge conglomeration owned over 42 theaters at the time in the tri-state district. The new owner completely renovated the theater, renaming it the Regent. The restored facility offered films, vaudeville, and personal appearances. The very first Veterans Memorial Service for the city was held in the theater on Sunday, November 11, 1923.

When it became obvious that the talkies were going to be permanent, sound was installed in the theater and a great variety of programs and features were added. In 1920, a weekly Friday night amateur program became a big attraction with local talent competing for a big prize. The theater closed its doors during the Depression, but in 1933, H. Goldberg of Pittsburgh formed a partnership with Fred Cook of Beaver and they bought the theater, remodeling it once again by installing lovely new plush carpeting, placing a huge statue of Romulus and Remus in the lobby and magnificent chandeliers in the ceiling, and reopening to enormous crowds.

The Regent quickly became the place where the city youngsters flocked each weekend to cheer on their heroes and boo the villains. The Regent became the home of the great grade-B westerns, jungle and action films, comedies, mysteries, and crime dramas. The Regent offered it all.

Who can ever forget impatiently waiting on a weekend afternoon outside until Mr. Reynolds Sr., the janitor, lowered the thin strand of restricting rope, and then racing inside up the enormously long lobby, past the imposing marble statue, pausing to fill up at the candy stand, and finally settling into the black confines of the auditorium? Then the weekly favorites would appear. A scream of outlandish proportions would greet the appearance of The Three Stooges, causing Reynolds to race backstage and hit the "silence" button, which no one paid any attention to. There would be films featuring Leo Gorcey, Hunty Hall and the Bowery Boys, Johnny Weismueller as Jungle Jim, Johnny Sheffield as Bomba the Jungle Boy, Ma and Pa Kettle, Francis the Talking Mule, and great war movies.

The Regent held contracts with Columbia, Universal International, United Artists, Monagrams, Republis, and Lippert Studios. That meant the Regent received all the weekly cowboy films. Local children were raised on Roy Rogers, Gene Autry, Johnny Mack Brown, and Charles Starett. We were treated to Allan "Rocky" Lane, Lash La Rue, Jimmy Wakely, Wild Bill Elliot, Whip Wilson, Monte Hale, Tim Holt, Rex Allan, and Rod Cameron. We laughed at Gabby Hayes, Smiley Burnette, Cannonball Taylor, Andy Clyde, Fuzzy Knight, and Andy Devine.

The Regent also showed prestigious westerns starring Glenn Ford, Forrest Tucker, Randolph Scott, Jimmy Stewart, and the greatest cowboy of them all, John Wayne. There would literally be lines of people stretching from the inside of the theater, outside and down the block and around the corner waiting to see *Sands of Iwo Jima*, *Fort Apache*, *She Wore a Yellow Ribbon*, or *The Quiet Man*. The other theaters in the city may have had more quality films and a better appearance, but the Regent had the people's hearts.

CINEMA THEATER. Cinema was formerly called the Regent Theater. Remember King's Jewelry Store or Jay's Bootery located to the right and left of the entrance of the old Regent?

But no matter how popular, the Regent also suffered from lack of business and closed its doors in 1957. It sat idle until 1963 when a local theater group called the Regent Players reopened the theater and presented live stage plays. *The King and I, Girl Crazy*, and *The Fantastics* were just a few of their endeavors. But again, lack of interest caused the theater to cease operations. Never giving up, the plucky showcase reopened as the Cinema in 1968 with the Rex Harrison film *Dr. Doolittle* as its opening attraction. It was fondly hoped that since it was now the only operating theater in the city, it would succeed.

But on March 2, 1980 while the movie *Godspell* was playing, fire struck the establishment and within a few hours, this home of so many happy memories and thrills was reduced to an empty shell that was never reconstructed and later razed. The Regent, the last and perhaps the greatest of all the city theaters, is now only a memory.

However, those four theaters were not the only entertainment centers in Beaver Falls. Through the years, there had been many other fabulous showplaces. During the early years of this century, the area from Ninth to 12th Street on Seventh Avenue was referred to as theater row.

Martin Metzgar, in a building at Ninth Street and Seventh Avenue, as early as 1900 showed the first slide pictures on a screen. In 1907, a small theater opened on the east side of Seventh Avenue between Seventh and Eighth Streets. Slides

GRAND THEATER. This well-known theater was located on the corner of Tenth Street and Seventh Avenue. You can also see the Evash Theater on the opposite corner.

were featured, but this time highlighted by piano music played by Mrs. Nell Coleman. Mrs. Coleman's daughter also sang appropriate selections. This theater lasted a year.

The Star Family Theater, presenting vaudeville acts, also opened about the same time at 1026 Seventh Avenue. Charles Beaver was the manager. The theater soon closed its doors in 1909. Another slide projection theater was Dreamland, which opened in 1909 and closed in 1911 when silent films became the rage. Dreamland was located at 918 Seventh Avenue.

More famous and long lasting was the Comet Theater, owned and operated by Floreny Roney and Emerson Latto at 1009 Seventh Avenue. This was the first so-called nickelodeon in the city, so named because admission was a nickel. The Comet ran all the latest silent films, including *The Perils of Pauline*, John Barrymore in *Dr. Jekyll and Mr. Hyde*, plus Saturday matinee Punch and Judy shows.

Also in 1910, the Ev-Ash Theater, another silent film movie house owned jointly by Charlie Everetts and Al Ashenbaugh and located at 1000 Seventh Avenue, came into being. In 1911, it became known as the Queen Theater under new owners Roney and Latto and it closed permanently in 1915.

One of the most famous city theaters was the Grand owned by John Strub and established at 1010 Seventh Avenue in 1911. This was a larger theater than the others and ran the more important films of the day such as *The Sheik*, *A Tale of Two Cities*, *Rebecca of Sunnybrook Farm*, and *The Mark of Zorro*. The Grand also boasted of having the largest curved mirror screen in the region. The screen was so huge that the back wall of the theater had to be torn down so it could be installed.

The Grand was the only theater in the city running continuous showings. The movies started at 1 p.m. and continued until 11 p.m. The admission was 5¢ and 15¢. Although popular, the Grand closed forever in 1924.

As one can easily see, Beaver Falls has a long history of outstanding theaters. In conjunction with the long history and association Beaver Falls has had with theaters and movies, it is understandable that the city has been host to many famous film personalities and lecturers and was the recipient of many of the old-time movie promotions.

During the 1930s and 1940s when movies were king and it was inconceivable they would not rule forever, the major studios devised many promotional gimmicks to plug their products. Usually it was the live appearance of a film star or several of the cast. However, once in a while, something more unique would be created.

The most obvious attraction to lure crowds to the theater was the stars themselves. Quite a number visited Beaver Falls over the years. Aldo Ray appeared at the Granada Theater to plug a war movie he was in and Pat O'Brien also graced the show place. However, the theater that boasted the largest number of stars was the Regent. Quite a few notable western stars greeted customers in the lobby. Practically every local citizen knows that the king of cowboys, Roy Rogers and the Sons of the Pioneers, put on a live program in 1941 from the Regent stage.

But it is not as well known that Hoot Gibson, Johnny Mack Brown, Wild Bill Elliot, and the famous Smiley Burnette dropped by to greet area fans. Also visiting were Jackie Cooper and the lovely Irene Dunne. Another outstanding western star that visited the area was Ken Maynard.

From time to time, local theaters also passed out autographed photos of featured stars. Many young people received pictures of Roy Rogers or Gene Autry. There may still be a few around gathering dust. Sometimes, Frank Buck handed out books written by the star, like when the Granada gave away copies of *Bring Em Back Alive* when his feature was playing.

During the late 1940s, local residents were thrilled and fascinated when a family of real Native Americans rode into town to promote a western film. They pitched their teepees on the grounds of the City Building and kept their horses quartered in the fire station. Needless to say, the movie drew big crowds.

The local theaters also enticed customers with giveaways, such as grocery baskets brimming with food to be given to someone holding the lucky ticket. Raffles were held and the local radio station would give away pairs of tickets to those correctly answering movie questions.

To promote a horror double feature, one night a magician was hired to present a stage show that drew a huge crowd. However, he was laughed off the stage when the monsters he produced were only the local ushers running up and down the aisle wearing glowing masks.

One time in front of the theater where a large crowd stood, there was a flatbed truck with a huge mechanical gorilla waving his six-foot arms and beating his chest while roaring menacingly. *King Kong* was playing and if that mechanical monster didn't make you want to see the movie, nothing could. Every kid in town went crazy, and the movie played to a packed house due in no small part to the gigantic, bellowing creature outside on the truck. Movie promotions were fun, but they weren't the only entertainment attractions that made headlines over the decades.

As previously mentioned, at the turn of the century, many outstanding stage performers appeared in the city. Lecturers have also passed through our streets and numerous organizations, such as the prestigious Pittsburgh Symphony, the United States Navy Band, and the Victor Artists of the Victor Recording Studios, have musically enhanced the city environment.

Many music personalities from a wide variety of fields have presented programs in Beaver Falls. Country-Western stars like Roy Rogers and the Sons of the Pioneers, Roy Acuff and the Smokey Mountain Boys, and Wilma Lee and Stoney Cooper were among the many who performed at the Regent. The Mason Troupe, the Duquesne Tamburitzans, The Lettermen, The Brothers Four, and Al Hirt have offered their talent to the city, along with Johnny Ray.

For a short time, the Regent was the home for professional wrestling and many great wrestlers grunted and groaned to the crowd's delight. World Champion Lou Thez, Jack Vansky, Bob Guidgel, Chief Don Eagle, Antonnio Rocco, and Ray Bently (a hometown professional) pulled in huge crowds. The Harlem Globetrotters also performed their magic here in the city.

GRANADA THEATER. Located in the 1100 block of Seventh Avenue, it is now the Mini-Mall Senior Citizens Center.

Such diverse personalities as former heavyweight boxing champion Primo Carnaro visited the city, as did other boxing greats like John L. Sullivan, who appeared at the Sixth Avenue Theater in 1892, Bob Fitzsimmons at the Elks Club in 1897 and 1899, and Jack Johnson in 1914. Baseball great Bill Mazeroski visited the city following his famous home run blast in the 1960 World Series accompanied by the colorful Pittsburgh Pirates sportscaster Bob Prince.

Over the years, Beaver Falls has been host to William Bramwell Booth, founder of the Salvation Army, who spoke at the Little Red Schoolhouse in 1888. Also speaking at the schoolhouse was Brigham Young, the Mormon Leader who came in 1845. General "Mad" Anthony Wayne and Aaron Burr also graced our district, along with Zachary Taylor. The famous strip tease artist Sally Rand also appeared in the city. Comedy western sidekick Fuzzy St. John, famous for his stutter and singing, who starred with Wild Bill Elliot, Jimmy Wakely, and "Rocky" Lane, had relatives in Beaver Falls and visited often.

The legendary aviator Amelia Earheart also graced our city when she appeared on the Geneva College campus on Friday, March 20, 1936 to speak on the future of aviation and women's roles in it.

Through the years there have been numerous local theater groups. During the early 1900s, the William Leuis Stock Company played a number of city engagements and also toured the country. Leuis was a respected professional local actor who appeared in plays with Edward Arnold, William Holden, Frederick

COMET THEATER. *Formerly called the Express Theater, it was located in the 1000 block of Seventh Avenue. This was the first so-called Nickelodeon in the city. Admission was 5¢.*

March, and Jason Robards Sr. He also performed with James O'Neil in *The Count of Monte Cristo*, acknowledged during its time as one of the most outstanding plays in the country.

During the 1940s, a group consisting of many locals, including Red Miller, Gerry Gaff, Mary Francis Gilchrist, Nancy Starr, and others, presented stage plays in the old Carnegie Library Theater. Their last production was *The Hasty Heart* in 1946. The Regent Players also performed from 1963 through 1966, featuring such local talent as Peggy Denison, Val Staley, John Hellman, Hank Gardener, and others.

Rudyard Kipling, the noted author who gave the world *The Jungle Book*, *Gunga Din*, *The Man Who Would be King*, and other masterpieces, rode over our surrounding hills and visited our local factories about 1865. He also made a brief speech here.

Another famous lecturer who presented a well-received number of programs over the years was legendary sportsman and big game hunter Wally Taher. He first came to Beaver Falls in 1954. Appearing before a packed house at the Regent Theater with his leopard-lined pith helmet and zebra-trimmed jacket, he captivated the crowd with his exotic films, resonant voice, and flashing smile. Taher and his associates brought their outdoor adventure films to the city for over 20 years.

Also bringing magnificent culture and entertainment to the city for many years was the community concert series, which brought some of the world's greatest performers to thrill local audiences. The association was first formed in 1936 and was highly successful, bringing a number of outstanding performers to the city, including famous Broadway star Ezio Pinza of *South Pacific*. Lack of interest and a drop in ticket sales stopped the series for a while in the 1950s and 1960s, but fortunately it was revived in 1970. The late Reverend Jim Gahagen and several others were instrumental in reorganizing the group.

At the present time, The Beaver Valley Concert Association is very strong and each year brings distinction to the city by presenting nationally recognized artists and entertainers. When the series opened for the 1971–1972 season, it had an operating budget of $9,800, yet succeeded in obtaining the services of the Pittsburgh Symphony Chamber Orchestra, Karen Armstrong, and the Norman Luboff Choir.

Over the years, Beaver Falls has been the recipient of such gifted, versatile artists as the George Shearing Quintet, Victor Borge, Mitch Miller, Peter Nero, Roberta Peters, Robert Merrill, John Raitt, John Gary, the Robert Wagner Chorale, Ferrientti and Tiecher, Pat Boone, and Florence Henderson. As long as the association continued, Beaver Falls remained a center for culture and the very best in entertainment.

If the old saying that the way to a man's heart is through his stomach is true, then a lot of hearts have been lost over the years in many of the city's outstanding restaurants.

Probably no other business becomes so identifiable with the personality of a city as a restaurant. There are the classy establishments with a refined atmosphere that cater to a particular clientele, the middle class eateries that have something for everyone, and the traditional "mom's" type restaurants where a certain group will gather day after day to partake more of the friendship and conversation than the food. Some restaurants featured a specialty or a certain type of cuisine that would make them famous, such as Italian dishes, seafood, tasty desserts, or perhaps a mouth-watering breakfast. Many were famous for the friendliness or efficiency of the staff or management. Whatever the attraction down through the years, Beaver Falls has had a wide variety of eating places, some of which have become a well known part of city history.

The name Lou Pappan is synonymous with good food and famous restaurants throughout all of Western Pennsylvania and sections of Ohio. Pappan created an empire of restaurant chains recognizable not only for their excellent menu, but for the friendly, down to earth personality of Lou Pappan himself.

"Chicken, chicken, chicken" and "You're gonna like it" have become the trademark expressions that immediately identify Lou Pappan. The warm smile, the easy grin, the seemingly boundless energy and enthusiasm, all gathered together in a truly affectionate personality encased in a short, Santa Claus–like body, project the image of "Uncle Lou." But like so many other self-made men, the beginnings of his success were hard and difficult.

Born in the Greek village of Makrakomi, Lou can recall the horrors and turmoil of growing up during World War II. He witnessed many deaths of family and friends from starvation and bombings. After struggling to become an architect, but failing to pass the entrance examinations, his uncle Lou Nellis sponsored him so that he could come to the United States. He arrived at Ellis Island on June 7, 1951, a frightened 20-year-old with a single suitcase and no ability to speak or write English.

He was eventually picked up by a cousin after standing for several hours with a placard in his hand announcing his name. He arrived in Beaver Falls three days later to live with the Nellis family for the next several years.

His uncle loaned him $700 for his voyage and Lou paid him back at $5 a week until the debt was paid. During those difficult years as he struggled to adapt to a new country and language, he worked on the garbage truck for the city, then for the local Belyea Aluminum while also working for his uncle. He also tended bar at the 26th Street Grill.

After serving in the army during the Korean Conflict, Lou returned in 1955 and became a bartender at the Broadhead Hotel and eventually co-owned the North End Hotel. The first step that would forge the future empire began in 1961 when Lou proudly opened the Sweet Shop on the main street. The name came from the fact that it was previously a well-known candy shop. The early menu featured an order of french fries for a dime, a soft drink for a dime, and seven hot dogs or hamburgers for a dollar. There are many city residents who can still remember Lou on his hands and knees personally scrubbing and cleaning the floors, mirrors, tables, and counters of his restaurant. Lou was never afraid to work hard to achieve his goals.

On his opening day, a city businessman, Joe Borneo, came in for coffee only to learn that Lou didn't have any money in the register to make change. Borneo smiled, walked out, and returned shortly with $40 worth of change to help Lou begin his first day. "I never forgot that," Pappan recalled. "All my friends and family, even strangers went out of their way to help me. Of course, there was more of a feeling of family in the community than exists now."

Good food, excellent service, and the determination of Lou soon transformed the Sweet Shop into a success. A lesser man may have been satisfied, but Lou had a dream, a goal. He firmly believed in the American concept that anyone could become as successful as he dared to. So within two years, he opened two local drive-in restaurants that were among the first of their kind. The novelty plus the good food and service made them highly successful. Lou was now on his way to success.

From there, he branched out into Pappan's Family Restaurants, which served a wide variety of meals throughout the Beaver Valley. He established eating locations in Beaver and Rochester, and the magnificent Pappan's Ark in Bridgewater. During the late 1960s, Lou continued to expand and in 1972, he bought his first three Roy Rogers franchises. Today, the Pappan chain includes 18 restaurants and 17 Roy Rogers Restaurants throughout western Pennsylvania that employs approximately 1,500 people.

In addition to his restaurants, Lou became famous for his annual senior citizens picnic hosted in Brady's Run Park. The first picnic attracted over 1,200 people.

A strong family man with a deep commitment to the traditional values, Lou has kept his business family-oriented in every aspect. His wife Patty is still his strength and foundation, while his son Demetrios is executive vice president, his son Spiro is the company treasurer, and his daughter Vasiliki represents the company after having graduated from the University of Dayton School of Law.

But for all his vast wealth and acclaim, Lou remained humble, never forgetting his early beginnings. He is intensely loyal to his friends and community. "I can never repay enough to this country and the people who helped me," he has stated and his generous donations and involvement in community projects prove this.

Even though his business has made him a recognized personality and a powerful, commanding leader in the business world, Lou's philosophy of life is still stated very simply: "I'd rather be known as a good man than a rich man."

Johnny's Restaurant, which was located at 915 Seventh Avenue, employed the slogan "Enjoy life, eat here more often" and for a lengthy time, many thousands of people did. Johnny's was one of the showplace restaurants of the city.

Formerly Zoes Restaurant, it was purchased in 1949 by John and Helen Slovak, who operated it successfully until 1962. The establishment was known county-wide for its excellent cuisine and wide variety of entrées.

Previous to his ownership, John Slovak had been the highly acclaimed master chef at the local Broadhead Hotel. Upon leaving the hotel, he and his wife opened Johnny's Restaurant on May 13, 1949.

SEVENTH AVENUE. The 1000 block has changed little from 1961 when Lou Pappan opened the Sweet Shop on the main street where Parker Vacuum is located at 1026 Seventh Avenue.

As is usually the case, the restaurant became successful only due to the extremely hard work and dedication put into it by John and Helen. John never had formal training, but was a born chef with an instinctive touch for how to prepare a meal. He was also an extremely warm, generous man who loved working with his staff and greeting his customers.

In 1962, due to poor health, John was forced to retire. The restaurant was then owned and operated by a brother- and sister-in-law until it finally closed in 1978.

Every small town in America had a local teen malt shop—a place to gather after school to meet friends, exchange gossip, sip a soda, talk about your latest heartthrob, and listen to the latest music. Such places are part of American tradition and culture.

Ice cream parlors were immensely popular at the turn of the century with entire families often going for a delicious early evening treat. Norman Rockwell featured ice cream parlors in his magazine cover illustrations. The cartoon strip "Archie" had the gang regularly meeting at the malt shop and, of course, the television series "Happy Days" highlighted such locations.

There were several establishments over the decades in Beaver Falls. The most famous and popular shop was Alps Ice Cream, which was known throughout the county for the excellence of its homemade ice cream. The business began in 1910 when A.J. Antill first started the operation. Within a year, his brother-in-law Theodore Gilchrist joined him. Before they began the ice cream parlor, the

JOHNNY'S RESTAURANT. The Slovak Family, who operated the establishment until 1962, purchased Johnny's in 1949. It is located in the 900 block of Seventh Avenue.

location had been a confectionary store owned by Edward Johnson. Eventually, Gilchrist bought out his brother-in-law and ran the business until his retirement in 1952. At that time, his two sons Thomas and John took over the operation.

Mr. Gilchrist manufactured his product from his own private recipe and gave the public a unique-tasting ice cream unmatched throughout the area. Crowds would jam the store, especially on a humid summer night either standing at the long counter or waiting for a comfortable booth that lined the walls. Old fashioned ice cream tables with the ornate iron chairs stood in the center of the floor. Mr. Gilchrist used to taste each batch of his ice cream making sure the flavor was just right. He jokingly said his expanding waist size was due to this habit.

One will never know how many romances bloomed or perhaps ended over the years in the confines of its walls. It was the favorite place to go after seeing a movie or attending a meeting. Young lovers would stare dreamily at each other while sipping a soda or indulging in the famous Alps banana splits or sundaes. Some just gathered for the good fellowship or to purchase some of the delicious homemade candy displayed in the long glass cases.

Very few individuals ever saw the rear of the store where all the hard work went into the preparation of the products. Here, the huge machines filled with cream that chilled and firmed the final product sat. The massive vats in which the homemade chocolate syrup was heated and made or the ice-enclosed freezer where the cartons of ice cream were kept before being delivered or sold were seldom seem by anyone but the employees.

But society changes and the economic situation became more difficult, forcing the business to eventually close. There were many heavy hearts filled with golden memories by city residents who had grown up in Alps when it closed it doors in late 1962.

Although not an eating establishment, for over 50 years the locally-owned John Kohlmann Bottling Company provided a wide, delicious variety of soft drinks that were a cool, refreshing thirst quencher for thousands of residents. The local company offered a wide range of flavors not easily obtained from the larger national bottling chains.

John Kohlmann, founder and president of the firm, was born September 15, 1889, in Froherkof by Niernberg in Germany. Having been trained in the brewing industry, he left his native homeland in 1912 and immigrated to the United States. He first settled in Warren, and then Pittsburgh before finally placing his final roots in Beaver Falls on February 12, 1917. He began working at the old Auderton Brewery the next day.

Prohibition brought an abrupt end to his employment and Kohlmann decided to open his own soft drink business. He obtained property and began the business on June 28, 1919. Kohlmann started out with a wooden washtub, a foot-power filling machine, and an old 1915 Ford truck. As time went by, he became more established and confident and began to expand and modernize his business. Within a few years, the company owned a modern wash machine, a Miller Hydrill

Bottle Washer, which washed 60 cases of bottles an hour, a bottle-filling machine, and a new carbonator.

During the early years, prices for the product fluctuated greatly depending on the price of sugar. At one time, a 24-bottle case of 7-ounce bottles of soda sold for 60¢, and maybe six months later it would cost $1. That was still a huge bargain even for those early times.

By 1920, Kohlmann was a recognized leader in the soft drink business and he began attending conventions around the country, always attempting to better his product. He and the company soon became known throughout the industry for the quality of their Soda Water. As the years passed, the business prospered, eventually growing into one of western Pennsylvania's largest soft drink distributors. This allowed Kohlmann to add more trucks, equipment, and staff, which was great for Beaver Falls.

In 1954, a major franchise called Royal Crown Cola and Nehi was added to the locally-produced varieties of soft drinks. This was followed in 1956 by the Squirt Franchise, in 1962 by Dad's Root Beer, and finally in 1963 by the Diet-Rite Cola Franchise. By 1960, the company had a staff of 34. It had 15 trucks and 5 sales cars and produced over 400,000 cases of soft drinks a year. They featured 69 products of various sizes.

Keeping the business in the family, Kohlmann's two sons John Warren and Jere R. were introduced into the business at an early age and both were made to work in every capacity of the trade before gradually becoming involved in management. According to German tradition, neither son was given any favors, but had to earn his position.

John Kohlmann, who was deeply respected and admired, passed away in November of 1971, at which time the two sons officially took over the business. The elder Kohlmann had been semi-retired for several years. The company continued, but changing times and taste, competition from the major lines, and even high production costs eventually forced it to finally close in 1979, leaving many Beaver Falls residents with only fond memories of a delicious-tasting local product.

One of the best-known combination dairy store and eating establishments was the Isaly's store at 1312 Seventh Avenue. Adults could purchase dairy products, cheese, luncheon meat, eggs, milk, bread, and soft drinks while youngsters enjoyed a large number of ice cream flavors, milkshakes, and sundaes. Hot lunches were also available. Isaly's offered something for everyone.

Isaly is the Swiss surname of a Mansfield, Ohio family that founded the chain of stores in the early 1920s. They pioneered the concept of franchising similar stores nationwide that merchandised dairy and like products.

The Beaver Falls Isaly's was franchised in 1927 to Harry N. Bricker, opening in a rented building at 1310 Seventh Avenue next to the flourishing Maggie Dambach's restaurant that was beside the Regent Theater. Four years later, it moved next door to a building erected especially for it. Dean Bricker, who bought the original franchise from his mother, added the College Hill store in 1946.

ISALY'S DIARY STORE. Clerks working at the store pose for a picture on May 29, 1949. From left to right are Sarah P., Katherine J., Bill, Catherine C., and Peggy P.

Both stores were highly popular meeting places for the public to eat and relax and for youngsters to gather after school to meet friends, have a milkshake, and play the jukebox. Some of the food specialties are still fondly remembered today, like the skyscraper ice cream cone made from any of the 16 different delicious flavors or the special klondikes (if you got one with a pink center, it entitled you to a free one). There was fresh-cut tub butter, imported cheese, fresh milk in bottles with the cream on top, and buttermilk, along with mouth watering chipped ham, huge dill pickles, three chocolate-covered Tip Top cupcakes for a dime, large bottles of pop for a dime, bread at a nickel a loaf, and a cafeteria service featuring hot meals, soups, and home baked pies.

But competition and lack of public support by the mid-1970s forced the company to declare liquidation and end the franchise. The company could no longer compete with shopping malls, fast food chains, and convenience stores. C.L. Bricker had closed the College Hill Isaly's in the early 1960s and, in 1967, Dean Bricker sold the downtown location back to the parent company. Thus came to a close another successful and highly popular Beaver Falls eating establishment that is now only a golden memory.

Throughout the years, there have been many places to eat that have been of outstanding quality and have held many fond memories for local residents. It is impossible to list them all, but a random sampling of some of these establishments over the years provided many names that should evoke countless recollections like ones that were opened in 1910 such as Anerson's at 1025 Seventh Avenue, Euarts

JOE TRONZO. Joe was one of The News-Tribune's *legendary sports writers. He was also noted for his witty observations and his ever-present cigar. Joe will be sorely missed by the entire Beaver Valley.*

at 616 12th Street, McGee's at 506 Seventh Avenue and Roney & Latto at 1011 Seventh Avenue.

During intervening years there were popular restaurants such as Joe's Café, the Sweet Shop, Johnny's Restaurant, Mary Laria's Spaghetti House, New Italy Restaurant operated by Angelina Magliochi, the Red Bull, Dolan's, Martins Restaurant, Dairy Queen, Wagon Wheel, Odlehour, and of course outstanding bakeries such as Oram's, Schomer's, Tomsic's, and the Doughnut Shop.

A widely known and popular brand of luncheon meat in the Pittsburgh area was Luger. That was the brand name of the meats produced by Peter J. Luger and Sons, Inc. at their plant in the Geneva Hill area of White Township, west of the Pennsylvania Railroad.

The 90th year the Luger family had serviced Beaver Falls and southwestern Pennsylvania with quality meats was celebrated in 1993. It was in 1903 that Peter J. Luger Sr. opened a retail meat market on College Hill. The wholesale meat-processing plant was begun in 1936 in a small building in the north end of Beaver

Falls, with Peter J. Luger Sr. and his four sons Paul, Eugene, Bernard, and Peter Jr. as partners. Steady growth of the business widened distribution of his meats until the marketing area covered all of Pennsylvania and bordering states.

By 1946, facilities were required to service the expanding business. A modern brick processing plant was built in White Township and the partnership became a corporation. Under the Luger label, the company originated such luncheon meats as Golden Maple Ham and Maple Turkey Ham. Other products include casing wieners, kielbasa, and the ever-popular Luger Jumbo Bologna.

The plant maintained a testing laboratory where every product was analyzed before it was sold and delivered, giving constant quality control on every product that was sold. The officers of Luger Meats in 1993 were Bernard Luger Sr., chairman of the board; Bernard Luger Jr., president; Ralph Zell, vice president; and Delores Stockman, treasurer.

Perhaps no single institution can become as important and identifiable with a community as a local newspaper. No other media has such persuasive power and the ability to manipulate, influence, or speak for the public as the press. This is an awesome and sobering responsibility. A reporter, through the judicious use of words, can slant a story or imply a subtle suggestion however he or she chooses. A reporter must at all times be alert to this possibility and refrain from succumbing to its temptation, however attractive. The job of a reporter is strictly to report the facts and not engage in speculation, innuendo, hearsay, or second-hand statements unless he so states that it is such.

If a newspaper wishes to take a stand on an issue or state its opinion about a topic that concerns the public, then it must do so in an editorial that clearly states that this is not a report, but an opinion. Fortunately, to their credit, most reporters and editors live by this responsibility and have the trust and respect of their readers. Throughout its history, Beaver Falls has had several newspapers with some outstanding writers.

At least three newspapers carried "Beaver Falls" in their names before a paper actually was published in the community—and the first one published here didn't have "Beaver Falls" in its name. According to Bausman's *History of Beaver County*, the *Beaver Falls Union/Beaver County Advocate*, published weekly by the Beaver Falls Press Association, was begun on January 6, 1838, with B.B. Chamberlin Esq. as editor. Bausman's report indicates it was published in Fallston with Chamberlin operating out of an office in New Brighton. The paper continued in operation until March 2, 1939.

The *Beaver Falls New Era* lasted but a few weeks after O.P. Wharton established it on February 28, 1866. It was printed in Allegheny and dated at New Brighton. The *Beaver Falls Chronicle* was the first paper in Rochester. It was started on October 12, 1839 with J. Washington White as editor and proprietor. It remained in Rochester until July 1840, when it was moved to Brighton (now Beaver Falls). Formally transferred to E. Burke Fisher on August 29, 1840, the paper received a new name—*Beaver County Palladium*—and was, according to Bausman, the first paper published in the town. The motto of the paper was, "take away the sword—the pen can save the state."

From December 12, 1840, the name of E. Burke Fisher disappeared from the paper and the prospectus was signed, "Publisher of *Beaver County Palladium*." In the issue of December 26, 1840, a notice for insolvent debtors appeared, signed by E. Burke Fisher and W.H. Whitney, late printers. William H. Eskridge and Company appeared at the head of the paper on February 6, 1841 and on March 19, 1841, the name of John B. Early appeared as editor. The paper was discontinued in the fall of 1841.

The first newspaper to be published in Beaver Falls and carry the town's name was the *Beaver Falls Courier*, which was started by John T. Porter in 1875. In the summer of 1879, he sold it to Roberts & Van Horn of Syracuse, New York, who changed its name to the *Beaver County Enterprise*. In 1880, Colonel Jacob Weyand purchased it and again changed the name, calling it the *Beaver Falls Tribune*.

It was in 1882 that Weyand sold to John H. Telford and W.S. Fulkman. One year later, Telford bought his partners' interest and continued the paper for a time as a weekly publication.

On August 25, 1884, *The Daily Tribune* made its appearance in Beaver Falls. It was the third daily newspaper in Beaver County. The newspaper was published at 623 Seventh Avenue. The editor's office in that original location was in the front of the first story of the two-story brick structure, and directly behind this room were the presses. Upstairs was the composing room and it was there that the reporters wrote their stories in longhand.

All material was set by hand in those days. Printers quit working on the newspaper about 2 p.m. or 3 p.m. and spent the remainder of the working day distributing type back into cases. The newspaper form was laid out in the composing room, then carried downstairs to the flat press. The type was used over and over again and after it had been in use for a couple of years, letters became worn and hardly legible.

It took two runs of the press to print *The Daily Tribune* and each paper was folded by hand. The front page came in plate form from Pittsburgh by express each morning. It contained world affairs (mostly days late), fiction, jokes, and such. The daily circulation was about 1,500. In 1890, the concern took the form of Tribune Printing Company, which was chartered on September 26, 1902.

About 1892, Telford purchased a two-story building at 623 Sixth Avenue and relocated his printing establishment. Practically the same plant layout prevailed at the new quarters until about 1909 when a one-story addition was built to the south for office quarters and a two-story addition to the rear for a pressroom on the ground floor, leaving the mechanical department on the second floor.

The Daily Tribune continued to publish under that setup until 1921 when it was sold to John L. Stewart and Tribune Printing Company was reorganized with Stewart as president, James H. March as vice president, and Frank H. Behringer as secretary-treasurer. The name of the publication was changed to the *Beaver Falls Tribune*. At the time of the sale, the "original" owners were Mrs. J.H. Telford, widow of the founder; John C. Telford; and Mrs. J.L. Houston. Following purchase of the paper, the new ownership gradually improved and augmented the facilities.

A growing intermingling of the interests of Beaver Falls and New Brighton, as well as increasing circulation, over-lapping of territory, and duplication of effort, led in 1928 to the purchase by the Tribune Printing Company of the equipment, subscription, and good will of *The Daily News*. On March 1 of that same year, the paper became *The News-Tribune*. Acquisition of *The Daily News* added some 10 years to the *Tribune's* historical background—*The News* having been established in 1874.

Major David Critchlow and Francis S. Reader founded the *Beaver Valley News* on May 22, 1874. They bought the material of the Beaver County Press. Reader was editor of the paper from the beginning and, in 1877, bought out the major's interest. He began publication of the daily *Beaver Valley News* on February 5, 1883. It was the first daily newspaper in Beaver County.

The News was Republican in policy and in 1878 its editor, while secretary of the Republican County Committee, prepared a bill passed by the legislature (which became law in 1879) governing Republican primary elections in the county—the first law of the kind in the commonwealth.

THE NEWS-TRIBUNE. *This local paper was founded in 1928 and the final edition was published on April 11, 1979. Their truck is photographed on Sixth Street just about where the telephone building now stands.*

The News plant burned in 1899 and was restocked and in operation just two months later with one of the "best outfits in the county." In January 1901, a Mergenthaler Linotype was installed—another first for the county. Increased business following the constant development of the community, reflected in the steady gain in circulation and advertising matter, soon presented a problem to management. A new press, designed to print more than 16 pages without a second operation, was seen as a necessity, but the building was neither large enough nor strong enough to permit installation of such equipment.

The composing room was overcrowded along with the job department. The mailroom facilities were inadequate also. These factors brought about planning in 1929 for erection of a new home for The News-Tribune. A plot of ground on the southeast corner of 13th Street and Main Alley was purchased from John T. Reeves and Company and, early in the summer, ground was broken for the building that has an Indiana limestone front and three stories. It was occupied on December 1, 1929 and improvements were made periodically as The News-Tribune kept pace with technical advances in the newspaper field, including the computer age.

Margaretta D. Stewart became the president of the firm in 1940 and her grandson William B. Northrop became chief executive in 1966. Mrs. Stewart continued in that capacity until her death in 1967. During her tenure, in 1945, the Beaver Falls Review was absorbed into The News-Tribune.

MARGE KELLER. Marge speaks to the College Hill Women's Club at The News-Tribune building on March 18, 1955.

The highly respected Mr. March continued as chief executive officer of the firm until 1971 when he was named chairman of the board of directors. Mr. March was a powerful, no nonsense executive who took a strong stand on issues and was deeply involved and committed to community affairs, and expected the same from his staff. He was hard but fair and usually put in more hours than some of his staff. He made his paper one of the most respected in the state. March retired in 1973 and died on Thursday, March 4, 1982 at the age of 88.

William B. Northrop became president of the firm in 1971. Along with his brother John, he became the prime stockholder and was the grandchild of John L. Stewart, who had purchased the company in 1921. Although Northrop continued to remodel and keep up with the latest advances in the printing industry, the company began to lose money at an alarming rate. Confronted with the reality of a failing business, Northrop and his brother decided to sell the firm to the *Beaver County Times*. The shocking announcement was made to the public in the final edition of April 11, 1979.

The sense of personal loss was heavy among local city residents as they expressed dismay at the unexpected closing of what was considered to be their paper. It was like losing a family member. Over the years, the local staff had become known, respected, identified, and even loved by loyal readers. Certain names conjured specific memories.

The writers wore many hats as they all covered various beats and stories. Even though some became closely identified with a certain field such as sports or community affairs, all were required to cover any local assignment. For many years, Tom Blunt, Fran McDaniel, and Luther Cornwell were recognized as the city editors and specialty writers. Don Coleman and Jim Stoner were also well known contributors. Although never a staff member, Susan Hoefling is fondly remembered for her freelance poetry offerings.

The sports department featured numerous outstanding writers and personalities that included Ernie Reid, Jack Henry, Johnny Ray, Ernie Konvolinka, "Scoop" Coates, and the irrepressible Joe Tronzo. As with most legendary sportswriters, over the years Joe would become as well known, if not more so than the sports he covered. Tronzo was always colorful chomping on his cigar stub while making witty observations.

Also not to be overlooked were the highly professional photographers who contributed so greatly to the prestige and character of the paper. Photos by Pete Pavlovic, Jimmy March, Paul Shell, and Walt Cianafarano would grace the pages and enhance many a local story.

Yet another well-known *The News-Tribune* personality was Billy McClain. McClain worked in the advertising department from 1939 until the final sad day of the final edition. McClain was an energetic friend to everyone in the city.

The *Beaver County Times*, which immediately acquired control, also had a long Beaver Valley history. Michael Weyland of Beaver founded the *Daily Times*, immediate predecessor to the *Beaver County Times*, on April 1, 1873. However, the present newspaper is a descendent of various periodicals that were published in

Beaver County's seat. Among these was the *Minerva*, which started in 1803 and is believed to have been the county's first newspaper. The *Daily Times* changed hands several times, but Weyland remained its editor until January 1, 1900. In the latter part of 1900, John L. Stewart and E.L. Freeland, both of Washington, Pennsylvania, purchased the paper and in July 1930, Freeland purchased Stewarts's interest and became sole owner.

In August 1946, Freeland sold the paper to S.W. Calkins of Uniontown, who in 1943 had purchased the *Evening Times* of Aliquippa. On October 16, 1946, the name was changed to *Beaver Valley Times* and later to *Beaver County Times*. In 1959, Calkins purchased the former *Ambridge Citizen* and the weekly *Ambridge New-Herald*, which were consolidated into the *Beaver County Times*. The *Times*'s current building is in Bridgewater and was dedicated on November 7, 1964. Calkins died at his office at the *Times* on May 24, 1973 and his son S.W. Calkins Jr. became president of the family-owned corporation.

Several other newspapers were also published over the years in Beaver Falls. In April 1882, W.S. Fulkman—who also published *The Spray* and *The Falls* in 1887 and 1888, both of which were short-lived—started the *Beaver Falls Index*. The *Beaver Falls Independent* was published in 1882, but was soon discontinued. W.F. Hanrahan and Frank A. Lewis were its first publishers and they succeeded W.W. Shields.

Globe Printing Company published a monthly paper, *The Globe Advertiser*, from 1875 to 1879. Later W.C. Fessenden and John Rohm changed it to a weekly publication. Others connected with it from time to time were Ed Hutchinson, G.W. Penn, and John Mellon. A morning edition—*The Herald*—was started, but soon failed. Mellon gained control of *The Globe* and consolidated it with the *Beaver Star* in 1887.

In June of 1888, J.E. McClure and J.W. Carson founded the *Evening Journal* and the same year, George Warrington began the *Psalm Singer*, a monthly publication. In 1889, Warrington and Carson became the owners of *The Journal* and in addition to the daily published a weekly, of which Warrington became the sole owner in 1890. In 1892, J.H. Irons and Smith Curtis took control of *The Journal*. In 1894, J.W. Carson and the Broadbent brothers bought Irons's interest and in 1895, L.L. Carson began *The Daily Record* in *The Journal* plant. *The Record* soon failed. In 1896, some New Castle newspapermen began *The Daily Republican*, but it was discontinued the same year.

J.W. Carson purchased *The Good Will*, continued the weekly edition and changed the name to *The Review* in 1897. *The Review* remained for a half-century before James H. Carson sold it to the Tribune Printing Company in November of 1845.

5. COMMITMENT TO EDUCATION

The first public school in Beaver Falls was built in 1837, three years after the Pennsylvania Free Public School Law was signed by Governor Wolf. It was more than a school, it was a civic center.

The law provided for a free public school system, but required election of a board of education to establish a school in each community. Beaver County joined statewide opposition to help delay election of such boards until some objectionable features were removed from the law in 1836.

An election was held locally in 1836 and a board was formed that began planning a school building. A two-room red brick building was erected at Seventh Avenue and Eighth Street and was used for the first time in September 1837. The school was built on land claimed by James Patterson and later Mrs. Patterson. It was conveyed to the school district in 1875 when $150 was paid for it.

This location was at the edge of town (Old Brighton). Before the school was built, children interested in getting an education journeyed across the river to attend a seminary conducted by a Miss Curtiss.

Known as the Little Red Schoolhouse, the brick building served as the only school in town for three and one-half decades. It also served as the town hall, a Sunday school room, a place for worship services and social events, and as a polling place.

The school board petitioned the state for a separate district for Old Brighton, which was granted in 1841. Sixty men signed the petition.

Reading, writing, and arithmetic were the order of the day at the Little Red Schoolhouse—there were no extras. Attendance was not compulsory. The first school board of which there is any record was composed of Robert Calhoun, John Baker, Thomas D. Wells, James Patterson, Archibald Robertson, and James M. Gregg in 1841.

The early teachers were men. The first woman teacher of which there is any record was Miss Kate Warren. William Robertson, James Robertson, Joseph Knotts, Christopher and Daniel Large, James Ross, Thomas and Margaret Hennon, Myra Reed, Adelaide Sims, and Rebecca McGahey were some of the early day pupils. Milton Anderson, a teacher, made the first known report on education in Beaver Falls in 1867.

ELEVENTH STREET PUBLIC SCHOOL. The all-in-one school was located on 11th Street and Sixth Avenue. Also known as the Union School, it was built in 1873. The bell tower and the third floor were lost in the fire of 1919, and the entire building was razed in the 1960s.

The Little Red Schoolhouse was the original home of most of the older churches in Beaver Falls and sisters of the Catholic faith conducted a parochial school there for a time.

In 1866, Dr. Thomas G. McPherson organized the first union Sunday school there. Among the congregation that had worship services there were Trinity United Presbyterian, First Methodist, the Methodist Episcopal, First Baptist, First Christian, and United German Evangelical.

Mrs. William H. Newlon, mother of Miss Helen Newlon (who taught many years at 11th Street School), conducted a night school there in the 1880s. Phased out as a school, the building was used as a warehouse and stable before Frank Poerlo Construction Company tore it down in 1928.

The Little Red Schoolhouse provided ample accommodations for the school district until the 1860s, just before Beaver Falls was incorporated. By 1866, the enrollment reached 239 pupils in 11 grades. From that time until 11th Street School was completed in 1873, rooms in various parts of town were rented and occupied for school purposes. The 11th Street School, when it was built, contained 10 rooms and a large public hall. In 1877, the hall was converted into two classrooms. When school opened in 1878, enrollment reached 837 and the building formerly occupied by Reformed Presbyterian Church was rented and occupied by the primary department.

Enrollment continued to rise and to meet the demand: the 17th Street School was built in 1880 and the Fifth Street School in 1882. In 1884, two additional rooms were added to the 11th Street building. The Eighth Avenue School was built in 1888 and the Fifth Avenue School was completed 10 years later when the school population exceeded 1,800 and the elementary system was on its way.

The system grew even larger and in 1894 and 1895, space was rented from English Lutheran Church to ease the situation. In 1907, the basement of the First Methodist Church was used for classrooms. Crowded conditions were relieved for a while in 1911 when a high school was built at 17th Street and Seventh Avenue. By 1915 and 1916, overcrowding again forced the school district to seek additional space and rooms in the second floor of Carnegie Free Library were used (which continued until 1931).

Eleventh Street School was badly damaged by fire on March 27, 1919, and classes were switched to nearby churches. Rooms in the Methodist Episcopal, First Methodist, (Calvary) UP and (Trinity) Presbyterian Churches were occupied by more than 400 pupils on school days through June 13, 1919.

The 11th Street building was restored, without its third floor, and classes resumed in the fall of 1919. Kindergartens were established at the 11th and 33rd Street Schools during World War II, culminating a project talked about as early as 1885. College Hill and Beaver Falls schools had been combined in 1931 when the area became the City of Beaver Falls. That added the 33rd and 38th Street Schools to the Beaver Falls elementary system and later, the College Hill Junior High, which later became a grade school.

Central Elementary was built at Ninth Avenue and 15th Street and South Elementary was erected on Fourth Avenue in the 1950s, giving the city the most modern facilities. An art supervisor, a music supervisor, physical education instructors, special reading teachers, and dental specialists were then added to the elementary staffs.

In 1958, Eastvale and White Township schools joined with the Beaver Falls district, some 16 years after negotiations began.

There are no known records to indicate the date Beaver Falls citizens first began to agitate for training for their children beyond the elementary school, but in 1877, the school board voted to establish a high school—the first secondary school in the county.

Miss Alice Abel, considered a most able and dedicated woman, was chosen "the teacher of high school." When she resigned in 1886 because of ill health, Miss Agnes Mackay was elected to replace her.

The first high school was located in the third story of the 11th Street building. It remained there until its second home was built in 1911. At first, there was only grade 11 in the high school, then there were two, 11th and 12th grades. In 1897 and 1898, when the "8–4" plan became standard, grades 9, 10, 11, and 12 made up the high school. Thirty-three students were enrolled in the first year of high school with only four boys attending. The average age was 16. To combat the problem of boys leaving school, M.L. McKnight, superintendent and principal, recommended a school/work program in 1882. According to his plan, boys would attend school half a day and work on a job the other half, but the board did not approve. Attendance in those days was still not compulsory.

In 1898 and 1899, 15 nonresident students attended the high school at a charge of $1.50 per month. In 1900 and 1901, there were 135 students in high school and Superintendent C.J. Boak urged construction of a new building. Principal G.G. Starr made a similar plea in 1905, but a year later, a motion by a board member to build a new school failed to carry.

Efforts resumed in 1910 were successful and a $700,000 two-story building with a full basement was built at 17th Street and Seventh Avenue. First occupied in 1911, the school had six classrooms and offices on the first floor, a study hall and four classrooms on the second floor, and a manual training department and large gymnasium in the basement.

Beaver Falls continued to grow rapidly, however, and within a dozen years, planning began for another high school building. In 1929, the school board approved plans for a new and bigger structure at Eighth Avenue and 16th Street. It was occupied in September 1931 and dedicated on October 1, 1931. This school

JUNIOR HIGH SCHOOL. Built in 1910 as the new high school, it became the Junior High in 1931. The building was razed in 1978 and is now the site of Wendy's, located on 17th Street and Seventh Avenue.

BEAVER FALLS ROLLER MILLS. Located on 22nd Street and Eighth Avenue, the roller mills were owned by John G. Allen. They were razed in the 1960s and the land is now part of the parking lot for the Tri-State Equipment Company and the Beaver Falls High School campus complex.

had 24 classrooms, a gymnasium seating 1,460, an auditorium seating 1,596, a cafeteria to seat 500, and a large library. The gym was the largest for a school in western Pennsylvania and the auditorium was the largest for a school in the state.

In 1936, Lester L. Fehr was named head of the general industrial arts program. Two years later, the name was changed to vocational shop program and the 17th Street building—formerly an elementary school—was used until an annex was built at the high school in 1949. The name was changed again to Industrial Arts with Donald E. Grove as supervisor. The program included shops in auto, machine, wood, electric, and graphic arts in addition to the agriculture program adopted in 1938. In 1961, auto shop was discontinued and agriculture was dropped a year later. The annex included mechanical drawing rooms, an art room, two classrooms, an office, and an elevator. A music room was added in 1963.

When College Hill split from White Township and became a borough in 1892, there was a two-room township school building at 33rd Street and Fourth Avenue. Two rooms were added in 1895 and in 1902, two more rooms were added, followed by two more in 1909. In 1915, the basement was remodeled. Ben Franklin of West Bridgewater, who was at one time the county school superintendent, was the first head of the College Hill Schools in 1892. There were two teachers on his staff. Teacher requirements were lax at first, but by 1907, the principal had to be a graduate of a normal school.

91

Students interested in attending high school went to Beaver Falls. There were six students in 1908. This persuaded the College Hill board to adopt a high school plan, but it was abolished in 1913 and students again went to Beaver Falls for high school. In the early 1920s, College Hill high school students attended New Brighton because the tuition rate there was cheaper than in Beaver Falls. In a year or two however, the rates were adjusted and students returned to Beaver Falls.

Plans for the 38th Street School were begun in 1908 and the structure was opened in 1915. In 1923, two rooms were added. College Hill Schools joined with Beaver Falls schools in 1931.

As early as the late 1950s, it was acknowledged by school administration officials that urgent plans for expansion or a new building must be considered due to overcrowding. Both Dr. Smith and Mr. Matthews recognized the oncoming crisis and began making tentative reference to the problem in their reports. However, both men would soon be gone, having retired from their positions before the situation finally demanded a solution.

The need to build a new high school had been a top priority since the Big Beaver Falls Area School District came into being on July 6, 1970. Following the Department of Education's approval of the district's long-range plan in 1971, the school officials engaged an engineering firm for a site location study. As the construction began and the vast expanse of ground was leveled and began to take

GENEVA COLLEGE. The old main building was completed for use in the fall of 1882 at a cost of approximately $35,000. The sandstone for the building was quarried on the site.

shape, excitement began growing not only among the administration, faculty, and students, but also within the community and among the city residents. A new school encompassing the history and records of the glorious past would combine with the new advancements and technology of the future. It was obvious the Beaver Falls school system was facing the challenge of the future, assuring the city that the school system would continue to be among the finest in the state.

Accordingly, it was a proud moment on Sunday, October 29, 1978 at 2 p.m., when the official dedication of the magnificent new edifice was conducted.

With authorization of Lakes Presbytery of Reformed Presbyterian Church, Geneva Hall (later to become Geneva College) opened its doors in Northwood, Ohio on April 20, 1848. A brick building containing five classrooms had been built and circulars describing the proposed college were distributed widely through the church. From the first, the college was co-educational and without racial discrimination. Especially after the Civil War, a considerable number of African-American students attended.

As solicitation of funds for the support of the college was carried on, agitation to have it moved eastward developed and the Reformed Presbyterian Synod of 1878 appointed a commission to study the question of its future location. The Synod of 1879 considered three possibilities besides Northwood: Beaver Falls, Pennsylvania; Bellefontaine, Ohio; and Morning Sun, Iowa. The majority favored Beaver Falls, provided that a grant of 10 acres and $20,000 for a building was made available. John Reeves Esq., on behalf of the Harmony Society, offered the land and various contributors pledged the required $20,000, and the college moved to Beaver Falls in 1880.

Today in McCartney Library may be seen the length of grapevine which the committee used in laying out the approximate position of the building. The outer shell of the building is of native sandstone quarried on the site. Since the building was not ready until the fall of 1882, classes were held for two years on the property of First Reformed Presbyterian Church of Beaver Falls, then located at Ninth Street and Seventh Avenue.

The board of trustees was reorganized to comply with Pennsylvania law and a charter was obtained in 1883. In 1887, part of Old Main was unroofed in a storm and required extensive repairs. A wooden building was erected in 1888 that was to be used as a gymnasium.

Rather early in Dr. Johnson's regime as president of the college, funds were obtained for erection of a science hall and the purchase of an athletic field. The science building was completed in 1896 at a cost of about $8,000. The athletic field, lying south of 33rd Street and west of the houses fronting on Sixth Avenue, was used for outdoor sports for about 30 years.

In 1910 and 1911, a brick gymnasium was built to replace the old wooden one. Reconstruction of the science hall, badly damaged by a fire in 1912, and a thorough remodeling of the auditorium made necessary by a second unroofing of that part of Old Main was done shortly after the brick gymnasium was completed.

This project was completed during 1914 and 1915, and included changing the balcony and providing the entire auditorium with opera seats.

Dr. Robert Clarke obtained a very generous donation from Mrs. M.E. McKee of Clarinda, Iowa, which enabled the college to build a women's dormitory—first occupied in 1921 and 1922. A few years later, Dr. Clarke persuaded former parishioners of Dr. Clarence Edward McCartney to finance a library building named in McCartney's honor. This beautiful edifice, with outstanding stained glass windows depicting *Paradise Lost* and *Pilgrim's Progress*, was dedicated in 1931.

When Dr. Lee retired in November of 1956, Dr. Clarke was elected to the presidency and was formally inaugurated in October 1957. In his 11 years as president, many changes have taken place. Fire-resistant stairwells have been provided for Old Main, the dining area of McKee Hall has been increased, two new dorms honoring Drs. Robert Clarke and M.M. Pearce have been erected, a spacious field house has been built, the capacities of the library and of the heating plant have been greatly enlarged, a magnificent student center is now serving the college, and work is underway to complete extension and remodeling of the $2-million science and engineering hall.

With the ever-increasing enrollment at Geneva College, more student housing was needed. A new structure named for Northwood, Ohio, the birthplace of Geneva College, was dedicated on April 26, 1998. Built between Old Main and Reeves Stadium, this beautiful three-story unit contains student housing, teaching facilities, and administrative offices. Also, through a bequest from Geneva alumni Dr. and Mrs. Claire Merriman, Merriman Athletic Complex has been built on the former Armstrong Cork complex at the foot of College Hill. Also, Alexander Hall, the new dinning room complex, was constructed in the late 1980s.

Carnegie Free Library of Beaver Falls has the distinction of being the first public library in Beaver County. To most people, the history of the library began when the doors to the present building were opened to the public in 1903. But the roots of this library reach back to a much earlier day when a group of prominent and civic-minded men gathered to form a library association for the purpose of establishing a public circulating library.

This occurred in the autumn of 1883. A year later, a plan to give a series of public lectures was suggested to a limited group of citizens meeting in the reading room of the engine house. It was decided to present six lectures in conjunction with the students of Geneva College. The profits were to be shared with Geneva, the manager of the Opera House, and the Library Association. The association's share was $60.86.

Quoting from a lecture given by M.L. Knight, superintendent of schools: "With $60.86 in the treasury, visions of a magnificent, brownstone, four-story building rose before our eyes in the misty future." Three results emerged from this effort. First was the definite organization of what was to be known as the People's Library Association with Julius F. Kurtz as the president. Second was the decision to maintain an annual lecture course that continued to flourish long after the present building was erected, and third was the establishment of a circulating library. This library, with a nucleus of 100 books, was opened on December 31, 1884 in Will Mitchell's grocery store, which was located on the corner of 13th Street and Seventh Avenue. The fee charged was $1 for two years or 1¢ a week.

The wish of the association was to open the 1885 and 1886 lecture course with Andrew Carnegie as speaker. Carnegie declined because of a business engagement. However, he sent a check for $100 with the intimation to call again.

Money accumulated very slowly. Donations of books and money were received, but by the first of 1887, there was still only $258.72 in the treasury. Because of this, an industrial display was planned. Beaver Falls had many and varied industries. This exposition was held in the Sixth Avenue Theater, the center of all cultural activities at the time. The affair was under the direction of Dr. H.C. Watson, a prominent citizen and a man with many interests, but chief among them was the establishment of a free public library.

It is interesting to note the variety of industries displayed. Among the firms exhibiting were Hartman Steel Company, Co-operative Flint Glass Company, Hubbard Company (with its display of chopping axes and cotton hoes), Beaver Falls Great Western Files Company, H.M. Myers Shovel Company, Mayer Brothers Fine China Company, Knott Harker Company (manufacturers of grates, marble, and slate mantels), Art Tile and Decorative Tile Company, Howard

CARNEGIE FREE LIBRARY. Located on 13th Street and Seventh Avenue, the outside appearance of the building has changed very little in the past 100 years.

COLMAN J. MIDDLEMAN AND WIFE MARCIA PEARLMAN MIDDLEMAN. For three generations, the Middleman family has owned shoe stores on Seventh Avenue. Marcia owns Original Nancy's Flower's at 1320 Seventh Avenue and also serves on the library board of trustees.

Stove Company, Beaver Falls Steel Company, Beaver Falls Glass, and Emerson Saw Company.

The exposition opened with a selection by the Merchant's Band, followed by an inspiring address by the superintendent of schools, M.L. Knight. In his talk, he stated, "It is the desire of the association to present to the public a class of literature attractive to all classes of people." After all the expenses had been paid, $700 was added to the treasury.

In January 1899, a committee composed of W.H. Morrison, J.F. Merriman, H.W. Reeves, and F.F. Brierly was appointed to contact Andrew Carnegie asking for a donation with which to build a library. Considerable correspondence ensued. Finally, a letter was received in which Carnegie offered a gift of $50,000 for the purpose of erecting a building suitable for a library.

The *Daily Tribune* of September 13, 1899, the day the letter was received, carried the following report:

> Beaver Falls is to have a public library. Andrew Carnegie, the iron king, has again shown his philanthropy. At noon today, William Morrison Esq. received a letter from Andrew Carnegie at Skibo Castle and dated

September 4, 1899, stating that he would give $50,000 for a library for Beaver Falls providing the people of the town would furnish the site and maintain the library.

Of course the offer was accepted. The committee immediately started to search for a plot upon which to locate the library. John T. Reeves offered a lot back of the old post office, where the present *The News-Tribune* building stands, but this plot was too small for the building they planned to erect. At last, the committee decided upon the present site at the corner of 13th Street and Seventh Avenue, where at the time Adolph Yokel's Shoe Shop was located. This shop was moved to 2411 Seventh Avenue.

The association had $1,500 in the treasury. This was augmented through solicitations and donations. Then, when plans and blueprints were prepared, it was found that more ground was needed in order to provide adequate lighting on the north side. Thirty more feet were added to the original lot, but the association still lacked $355 of the needed amount and John Reeves made up the deficit. Thus, the purchase was closed with the property owners, Cynthia and Sarah Reeves. The total purchase price was $14,000. The additional 30 feet made it possible to place the building 24 feet from 13th Street and 10 feet farther north than was planned.

The next step was to arrange for maintenance of the building. Borough council was approached, but did not wish to be obligated. The committee next visited the school board. After several meetings with the board and much correspondence between Andrew Carnegie and the school board, an agreement was reached. Carnegie was not willing to give the money until he was assured the library would be adequately maintained. It was not until November 13, 1900 that Carnegie wrote that the agreement with the school board was satisfactory. The board agreed to maintain the building and provide appropriations for books and salaries, provided it was represented on the library board. The president of the school board and the superintendent of schools always have been members of the library board. The school board explained its reasons for assuming the responsibility with these words: "The placing of a free public library in Beaver Falls would be a public benefit and of great advantage to the educational interests of the Borough of Beaver Falls."

The library was first opened for inspection in June 1903, and the reading and reference rooms were opened on September 21. On December 17 of that same year, the first books were circulated. To appreciate the growth of the library, and to realize its need for expansion, compare the statistics of various periods. In 1884, the circulating library had 100 books; in 1904, the books numbered 2,872; and today, the total number of books is almost 60,000 volumes. The circulation for 1904 was 11,978 and the daily average was 94. Today, the annual circulation is up to 64,000.

In the early days, 62 magazines were available to the public in the reading room. Today, there are about the same number, but added to that collection is the magazine database on the computers. The newspapers have not varied much. Six papers were taken in 1904 as compared to about 12 today.

Through the 100 years of the library's existence, several people have served as head librarians. Miriam Morse was the first librarian. Hazel Clifton (Mrs. J.D.P. Kennedy) served from 1905 until 1917, and Elsie Rayle from 1917 until 1956. In both World War I and World War II, the librarians Miss Clifton and Miss Rayle did outstanding work collecting, packaging, and sending books to our boys in camp. Fern Medley was next in line to serve as head librarian, but had to resign in June 1966 because of ill health. Abdul Aziz Khan of Pakistan became head librarian on March 1, 1967. In 1975, Nell Thomas served as head librarian until 1977 when Karl Helicher took over the position. In 1981, Elizabeth Spiro became head librarian and was followed by Linda Focer Taddeo, who served for about 17 years. Today, the head librarian or director is Jean Ann Barsotti, who took the position on March 12, 2001.

The first Carnegie Free Library Board held office in 1903 and 1904, and included the following members: A.J. Jolly, George W. Altsman, G. Fred Siemon, Dr. James S. Louthan, Edward L. Hutchinson, John A. Snyder, Joseph D. Strock (who was also president of the school board), Edward Maguire (superintendent of schools), and Charles F. Bond, who also served as school district treasurer.

It is interesting to note that in the days of the library association, only men were members. This also was true of the library board until 1937 when the first woman was elected as a trustee.

Many changes have been made as time passed. There was a period when patrons were permitted to take out only one or two books at a time. Since the book stock has been added to from year to year, these restrictions have been removed.

The library building, in addition to housing books and magazines, has also served many other purposes. The entire second floor was being used for all the eighth grade pupils of the public schools during the years of 1916 to 1930 or 1931. Later, after a fire in the Eighth Avenue Building, these rooms were again used for school purposes. Today, these second floor rooms are used to house the Beaver County Research and Resource Center for Local History, which is under the direction of Bill Irions and Betty Conners.

The basement on the 13th Street side did not served any practical purpose for several years. A public restroom eventually was established and maintained by the city. For a number of years, a senior citizens group met in one of the larger rooms in the basement until it disbanded in 1991. Now the city historical museum is housed in one large section of the basement.

Appreciating the great need for expansion, the board of trustees sought a solution to the problem. Someone presented a plan for a new building on 11th Street and Sixth Avenue. The trustees dismissed this as impractical. Already, they had considered that the logical space to be used would be the auditorium. For many years, this had been the cultural center of Beaver Falls and was a source of income for the library. After the erection of the present high school building with its modern auditorium, the one at the library became a liability to maintain rather

MARCH PARKLET. Erected in 1986, it enhanced the exterior of the library. This lovely parklet was named in honor of James H. March Sr.

than an asset. The opportunity arose to rent the auditorium to the Pennsylvania Bureau of Employment Security. They wanted to use the space for offices providing the room could be converted to suit their needs. Discussions developed as to what remodeling would be necessary for both the Employment Security Office and the library. One change that occurred from these discussions was the floor, which sloped from the rear of the room to the stage. It was raised to be level with the floor of the library.

The Employment Security Bureau paid for the expenses incurred through the rental of the room and a substantial sum remained to help with the present improvements. The auditorium was rented with the understanding that if the board was able to remodel, the Bureau of Employment Security would vacate after sufficient notice. The changes needed were planned over a long period of time.

Welcome aid came in June 1962 when the state granted money to improve library services. This grant was to be used for books, salaries, and equipment. Trustees had accumulated money to be used for remodeling. It meant a great deal when, through a federal grant under the Library Service and Construction Act, the library found out that it might receive 49 percent of the amount needed if it could supply the other 51 percent. There wasn't sufficient money to cover the 51 percent, however. The school board arranged to loan the money needed to meet the deficit because the library did not have borrowing power. The money was repaid by making annual payments to the school board. Frank J. Dickerson was named as architect and the improvements were made.

The present library is a blending of the old and the new. Its wealth of material of past years, together with the best of the latest fiction and non-fiction, fills the shelves. Copies of the local newspaper are kept on microfilm in the Research and Resource Center and videos are also a part of the library's service to the public in striving to keep up with current trends. The library also has many computers connected to the Internet for public use. Instruction for the Internet is also provided. There is a used book sale once a month on the second floor.

The passing of Miss Medley, whose warm welcoming smile made many friends for the library, saddened the library family as well as the public. The public reading room has been furnished and decorated as a memorial to Miss Medley. A painting of her hangs in the library also. The money provided to establish this memorial came from the school children of Beaver Falls and other friends.

The library is constantly striving to improve itself and its appearance since it is one of the true landmarks of the city's existing skyline. Since 1984, a new furnace, roof, and front steps were added along with the repair of the side steps. During this period of renovation, the building exterior was cleaned and painted and the original windows were repaired while the lobby, children's rooms, office, and lounge were carpeted. The children's program room was also painted, carpeted, and furnished through gifts from Mrs. Louise Haefling and Dr. and Mrs. W. Clair Merriman. An elevator has also been installed which makes the library handicapped accessible.

In 1986, the building of a lovely parklet adjacent to the building enhanced the exterior. Comprised of trees, benches, and a water fountain, it was dedicated to the memory of *The News-Tribune* founder and editor James H. March Sr., and was named in his honor.

Several years later, the Beaver Falls District Authority placed three new lighting fixtures in the parklet as one of their city projects. The Carnegie Free Library continues to serve the needs of education, pleasure, and recreation through its many books, magazines, programs, and involvement in the community.

6. When the Nation Called

In 1776, our valley and what would become Beaver Falls was largely unknown and sparsely populated. It was subject to constant Native American attacks and intrusion of British forces. It was in 1778 that the newly formed American forces at Fort Pitt ordered the construction of Fort McIntosh at the present site of Beaver. Eventually, as the area was cleared of enemy forces and made safe, the famous fort crumbled and fell into disrepair. Sporadic fighting would continue until late 1793 when General "Mad" Anthony Wayne, who had made his winter encampment at Logstown near Economy, crushed the remaining hostile natives once and for all at what became known as the "Battle of Fallen Timbers."

It can never be known for certain how many area settlers fought and died during this period of our nation's history. However, old records provide the names of some soldiers by districts—Arthur Ackles and Joseph S. Line, Big Beaver; Thomas Beatty, Samuel Brown, James Craig, Thomas Davis, Joseph Douthitt, Hugh Gaston, George Shillito, Henry Woods, and Robert Wilson, all from South Beaver; Thomas Stratton, Chippewa; and Stacy Daniels from Beavertown.

The following are gravesites of known soldiers from the Revolutionary War. In the Old Stone Church Cemetery in Chippewa Township lie Matthias Shanor who died in 1807, and Thomas Stratton who died in 1846; in the White Reform Cemetery in Darlington Township lies Alexander Silliman; and in the Wilson Cemetery between Darlington Lake and New Galilee lies Ethan Cory, James McKim, and two unknown soldiers.

The War of 1812 is regarded by many as mainly a naval war, especially with the heroics of John Paul Jones and his famous encounter on Lake Erie. But it was during this brief but violent war that the British invaded Washington, D.C. and burned the White House. This war also saw the brilliant victory by General Andrew Jackson at the Battle of New Orleans.

Although our region was untouched by the war, some of our residents and settlers were involved. Upon learning of the capture of General Hull's army at Detroit, the local militiamen quickly organized for action. Showing their fervent patriotism, close to half of the eager men volunteered to march to Cleveland with $1,000 for expenses and supplies for the 130 persons included in the party. Within two days, it is documented that the two companies had traveled from Beaver to Youngstown, but unfortunately all records of what happened to the expedition that was to have joined General Wadsworth at Cleveland have been lost.

On record as far as having served during this war from the Beaver Falls and Koppel area were Robert and William Duff, John Marshall, John Whampin, Alexander J. Scroggs, William McCullough, William McKim, and John Taggert.

The Mexican War was such a brief episode and occurred at such a far distance it is extremely doubtful that any son of Beaver Falls ever engaged in any action. If one did, there are no records to substantiate the claim.

The Civil War was the most terrible period of American history. The nation was torn apart and divided by war over bitter governmental issues. Father against son, brother against brother, husband against wife, the bloody war tore families apart and created attitudes and hatreds that persist to this day.

When the war broke out, the city of Beaver Falls as such was not in existence. Bitter lawsuits between the heirs of General Broadhead and James Patterson

JOSEPH MCCABE. This is our famous Civil War soldier. Many of Joseph McCabe's personal items are on display in the Beaver Falls Museum.

would continue to be contested until 1866. New Brighton at this time was the center of the upper Beaver Valley and our future city across the river was still referred to as "Old Brighton," consisting of two factories and perhaps a dozen or so homes.

During the first two years of the war, New Brighton sent five full companies of volunteers into action. Many of those volunteers would be from the area later to become our city. Practically all of our local volunteers saw action with either the Army of the Potomac or the Army of the Cumberland during some of the most terrible bloody battles in warfare. Men from our region fought at Vicksburg, Gettysburg, and Bull Run where losses of 5,000 to 10,000 in a single battle were not considered unusual.

Visit memorials and sections in area cemeteries and read the inscriptions on silent tombstones that bear eloquent testimony to the horrible toll of death and casualties that resulted from the Civil War here among our area residents. In the Beaver Falls and Koppel area, the records state that 252 soldiers were laid to rest.

Not all of our local volunteers saw service in the army. A few served in the naval forces, including Lieutenant Commander James P. Robertson of Beaver Falls, who served on the newly constructed ironclad *Kearsarge*, which did battle against the Confederate warship the *Merriman*.

Shortly after the war concluded in 1865, Beaver Falls was created from Patterson Township. Large numbers of war veterans became established in the newly formed borough and soon organized Post 164 of the Grand Army of the Republic (GAR). The post was organized through the period of 1880 to 1885 and conducted its meetings on the second floor of the Carnegie Free Library.

There were still hundreds of local veterans alive to participate in the Beaver Centennial of 1900, but gradually the soldiers took their final roll call and passed on. David Penney was the last Beaver Falls survivor and his last appearance was in 1938. He died two years later in 1940, only a year before our entry into World War II. The life of David Penney clearly demonstrates how young the United States, as a nation, truly is. Penney's parents were born shortly after the War of 1812. David himself fought during the Civil War and lived to see Hitler dominate all of Europe. It makes one realize that the Civil War still isn't so far removed from current history.

There are no records indicating what participation, if any, was conducted by Beaver Falls residents during the great Western Plains Wars. Undoubtedly, a few did see service on those vast prairies and treacherous gulleys and mountain ranges, but we have no record of it.

We do know many soldiers, who fought and died with Custer at Little Big Horn, were from the immediate area. There were 69 Pennsylvanians in Custer's 7th Calvary, including 9 from Pittsburgh, 1 from Oil City, and 2 from Lycoming, Lancaster, and Chester Counties, and 3 from Clarion.

With so many men serving in the west from such close proximity, it would indicate at least a few Beaver Falls men must have also seen action, but it appears we'll never know.

Whenever one visualizes the Spanish-American War, we immediately think of Colonel Teddy Roosevelt and his Rough Riders charging up San Juan Hill. Teddy and his men received all the headlines and glory from that brief encounter, but there was much more to the campaign than that single episode, and local soldiers were deeply involved in much of the action.

Except for meetings of the various posts of the GAR, there was no military activity organized until the formation of the New Brighton Guard in 1879, when Company B was the only unit in all of Beaver County. Two years later, there were Companies B, D, and E from New Brighton, Freedom, and Bridgewater. These units were transferred from the 15th Regiment to the 10th Regiment. The whole regiment served during a labor strike in April 1891 in Westmoreland County and again during the Homestead Riots of 1892.

At the beginning of the Spanish-American War, the 10th Regiment was in command of Colonel Alexander L. Hawkins. It first assembled at Mt. Gretna on April 28, 1898 for intensive training. Although the first order from Washington directed the movement of the regiment to Georgia for an invasion of Cuba, the order was changed to an assignment to San Francisco as part of the command of General Merritt to operate in the Philippines. As the troops passed west across Pennsylvania, they received great demonstrations at every station. In New Brighton, each man received a New Testament at the railroad depot before leaving. After eight days on day-coaches, the regiment arrived in San Francisco, then sailed on June 14 aboard the S.S. *Zealandia* for Honolulu. After another rousing reception, the convoy arrived outside Manila on July 21 and pitched camp in the suburbs. Meanwhile, additional troops had been recruited in the hometowns of the companies in western Pennsylvania to increase the size of the companies to the required strength of 106 men apiece. These recruits did not arrive until December 2, 1898 on the U.S. transport *Arizona*.

For the original group at Manila Bay, action suddenly began on July 31, 1898 and extended amid a typhoon throughout the night. Colonel Hawkins left his sick bed to lead his regiment, which earned the nickname of the "Fighting Tenth" in this first engagement. The local Company B was assigned to duty on Corregidor Island at a hospital area, where it remained until May 14, 1898.

Most of the regiment engaged in fierce fighting until the Spanish were defeated and the insurgents subdued. The 10th Regiment sponsored a baseball team with J. Edgar Boyle as catcher. This team won over all opposing regimental teams. It defeated a Japanese cricket team at baseball by the score of 15-5 en route home with stops at Nagasaki and Yokahama in Japan. The death of Colonel Hawkins at sea saddened the otherwise rejoicing regiment.

At San Francisco, a citizen's committee from western Pennsylvania met the 10th Regiment with funds from the home area plus $25,000 from the Pennsylvania Railroad to provide three special Pullman trains. The regiment arrived in New Brighton on August 28, 1899 in time for breakfast and then continued to Pittsburgh for a military and civic parade, followed by an official welcome from President William McKinley in Schenley Park. Later on September

30, the 10th Regiment marched in New York City at the "Dewey Day Parade" behind a 200-piece band led by John Philip Sousa. At the reviewing stand, Admiral Dewey gave them a special salute by removing his hat as the regiment passed. The men dressed in their battle uniforms of khaki breeches, blue shirts, and frayed campaign hats, and were in direct contrast to other outfits in full-dress uniforms.

The 10th Regiment were the first American troops under fire in the Philippines, the first unit engaged in Pacific jungle fighting and the most-traveled unit in American military history up to that time. The basic pay of a private was $13 in gold. The Spanish-American veterans received no hospitalization benefits until 20 years after their service. The travel pay and allowance provided for the Regular Army held up until 1941, when most of the soldiers were past 60 years of age.

Annual reunions were held in the various hometowns of the companies, one in New Brighton in 1950, with the most recent in Pittsburgh in 1962. The last

GAR MONUMENT. The Grand Army of the Republic Monument on Sixth Avenue and 10th Street was dedicated on February 10, 1913.

55TH ROTARY ANNIVERSARY. Taken in 1974, from left to right are Dr. George Carson; C.J. Melroth; Myer Berkman, charter member since 1919 and veteran of World War I; and Walter Broadhurst.

survivor in the City of Beaver Falls was William A. Lewis, who not long ago died after an illness in Deshon Hospital, Butler.

World War I was supposedly the war to end all wars. Instead, it ushered in a new, more frightening method of warfare and introduced soldiers to the nightmare of modern, high technology weapons that turned the art of war into mass murder: machine guns, grenades, tanks, air attacks, and rapid repeating rifles, all of which could decimate hundreds of men indiscriminately.

This was the terrible conflict that introduced the horror of trench warfare, where progress was measured in feet and a gain of 20 or 30 yards was heralded as a major victory. It was the first war to involve the world at large and it exhibited the very worst base instincts of man.

This was the war that exposed young American men to foreign travel and experiences in a scale of thousands. After confronting European cultures and lifestyles, these men would return home more sophisticated and mature with a different viewpoint and observations of our own way of life that would change and affect our nation forever.

This war would be the testing ground and would provide invaluable training for the future great generals such as MacArthur, Marshall, Patton, Bradley, and Eisenhower. It presented us with heroic personalities such as General "Black Jack" Pershing, Fighting Father Duffy, and of course Sergeant Alvin York.

If this was the war to end all wars, it failed miserably. But it prepared us for the horrors to come and gave us a new sense of identity and confidence in ourselves as a nation, and as always, Beaver Falls men were in the thick of the battle against dictatorship.

After the Spanish-American War, the 10th Regiment resumed its place in the National Guard of Pennsylvania. It was on duty in the hard coal strike of 1902 at Shamokin, was chosen to attend the inauguration of President McKinley in 1901, was selected to attend the dedication of the new Pennsylvania State Capitol in 1907, and was honored to appear (in full-dress uniforms) at the Philadelphia Centennial Celebration of 1908. During the tensions with Mexico, the regiment moved from Mt. Gretna to positions along the border in New Mexico and Texas for war maneuvers. It returned home to Pittsburgh on October 11 for a wild ovation, followed by a parade and a luncheon.

Since the 10th Regiment included units from the Beaver Valley, with companies from Beaver Falls and New Brighton, and already had its record from the Spanish-American War, it should be considered first.

The regimental commander was Lieutenant Colonel Henry W. Coulter, First Battalion commander was Major Joseph H. Thompson of Beaver Falls, Company B commander was Captain William Fish of New Brighton, and Machine Gun commander was Captain J. Edgar Boyle of Beaver Falls. The regiment was activated July 5, 1917; then on October 17, it was reclassified as the 110 U.S. Infantry. The local regiment arrived in Camp Hancock, Georgia and underwent a comprehensive training program prepared by Major Edward Martin. On May 3, 1918, this regiment sailed in a convoy from Hoboken, New Jersey, landed at several English ports on the western shore, moved across the island, and sailed from Dover to Calais, France.

The local Company B was first involved in the Battle of the Marne. It suffered severe losses when the French forces on both flanks retreated and left it exposed to attack on three sides. As part of the 28th Division, it participated in the Aisne-Marne Offensive, the Fieman Sector, the Oise-Aisne Offensive, the Neuvilley Sector, the Meuse-Argonne Offensive, and the Thiacourt-Metz Sector. Later evaluations by the Germans placed this 28th Division among the four best American divisions on the Western Front.

It was during this period of intense action that Colonel Joseph Thompson became the only Beaver Falls resident thus far to earn the Medal of Honor due to his outstanding bravery under fire. His actions that day in far-off France became legendary.

Joe Thompson was a quiet, unassuming man who was born on September 26, 1871 in Kilkeel, County Dawn Ireland. His family arrived in Beaver Falls two months after his birth to settle and establish a new home. Joe grew up to become recognized as a local athletic hero, lawyer, politician, and community leader, but above all an unforgettable war hero.

At the time of his action, October 1, 1918, Thompson was a major and the encounter occurred near Apremont, France involving his unit, the 110 Infantry, 28th Division. During heavy, intensive fire that day, two regiments of German troops counterattacked Thompson's battalion. Major Thompson continually encouraged his men in the front line, constantly exposing himself and braving the hazardous, consistent fire of enemy machine guns and artillery. His courage and example were mainly responsible for the eventual heavy repulse of the enemy troops. Later in the action, when the advance of his assaulting companies was held up by fire from a concealed machine gun nest and all but one of his six attacking tanks were disabled, the major single-handedly rushed forward on foot on three separate occasions in advance of the assaulting troops, under severe machine gun and anti–tank gun fire, and personally led the remaining tank to within a few yards of the enemy gunfire, which succeeded in eliminating it, thereby making it possible for his troops to advance and break the enemy line.

In the roll of honor, Colonel Thompson received the Congressional Medal of Honor, while Captain Boyle received the Distinguished Service Cross. Following duty as part of the Army of Occupation, the regiment returned to the United States on May 11–12, 1919, proceeded to Fort Dix, and took part in the "Welcome Home Parade" on May 14 in Philadelphia. Casualties of the 110th Regiment were listed at 4,183, or 112 percent of rated strength.

The other local unit in World War I of considerable strength from this vicinity was the 323rd Regiment of Field Artillery. The first quota of men from Beaver, Butler, and Washington Counties were assigned to Camp Sherman in Chillicothe, Ohio in the fall of 1917. Local men rode in day-coaches from Rochester and Beaver by way of Cincinnati, Ohio to the training camp. The officers had been previously selected from the Officers' Training School at Fort Benjamin Harrison, Indiana, so that local men numbering 764 had almost no possibility of becoming officers. Only one soldier, Clarence D. Frazier of Beaver Falls, was a second lieutenant. Other groups, chiefly from Ohio and Kentucky, joined this regiment.

The late fall and cold winter were devoted to concentrated instruction and drill and featured makeshift equipment, such as wooden guns, until equipment could be obtained. For example, the regiment used two Russian guns from the Crimean War and two guns from the Spanish-American era until modern guns arrived. However, the outfit made rapid progress and broke camp in June 1918 for action in the European War.

The 323rd Regiment landed at Le Havre, France for two additional months of training by experienced French officers in the operation of the lighter, but highly effective, 75mm artillery to be used in action. The first firing of artillery happened on October 8. Other action occurred in the support of infantry forces at Belleau Woods and in the Meuse-Argonne campaign. On November 11, 1918, the unit was positioned at Ecurey. After a pause for re-outfitting and inspections, it crossed the Rhine River as part of the Army of Occupation. Following months of rumors

COLONEL JOSEPH THOMPSON. Colonel Thompson received the Congressional Medal of Honor in World War I. He was also a local athletic hero, lawyer, politician, and community leader.

and uncertainty, the regiment was ordered out of Germany to Brest for return to the United States. The voyage on the *Von Steuben* consumed eight days before the landing at Hoboken, followed quickly by demobilization at Camp Merritt and discharge from Camp Dix on May 21, 1919.

This 323rd Regiment served exclusively in World War I, while the parent 83rd and 32nd Divisions functioned again in World War II with distinction. The regiment had a headquarters company, six batteries from A through F, a supply company, a medical detachment, and a veterinary detachment. Some specialists were wagoners, horse-shoers, saddlers, and blacksmiths since the artillery was transported on wagons or carriages by teams of horses. Most of the local men were in Batteries A through C with some in the other companies of the regiment. One member of Company B from Beaver Falls, Enrico Fusette, was killed in action and was awarded posthumously the French Croix de Guerre.

Since the tempo of the war had reduced the enrollment of men in colleges, most colleges made efforts to provide facilities for military units during the critical months of late 1918. Geneva College in Beaver Falls secured a unit of the Student Army Training Corps in October of that year, and almost 100 applicants, mostly former male students at the college, reported for duty. Since equipment and uniforms had not arrived on schedule, the men were given jobs of cleaning and painting in Old Main, and the project of converting the two halls of the literary societies into army barracks.

The program of studies arrived the day before classes were scheduled to begin, and confusion and frustration continued from day to day. The combination of army drills and classes did not proceed smoothly, and the college authorities and army command clashed most of the time. In fact, the missing equipment and uniforms did not arrive until after the Armistice. This experiment was ended on December 17, 1918 by the discharge of the members of the unit. The college gained valuable scientific equipment, dining room and kitchen equipment, new electrical wiring and fixtures in Old Main, and the free painting of several rooms. Indirectly, the government learned the weaknesses of these college programs, which would be corrected in future times of emergency.

Life at home had to be adjusted to meet the needs of the war activity. In the local book *History of Beaver County Home Activities During the World War*, George Hemphill prepared a report of the contributions on the home front. He mentioned campaigns for the five Liberty loans, the sale of War Savings Stamps,

FIRST WARTIME DRAFTEES. Early in 1942, the first draftees gather at the Pennsylvania Railroad Station before leaving for Odenton, Maryland. Louis Theurerl would be one of the first to be killed in World War II.

the raising of a War Chest for welfare organizations, collection of clothing for Belgian relief, gathering of fruit stones for charcoal in gas masks, free meals served to soldiers passing through the area on truck trains, and the making of hospital supplies. Important groups were: Local Draft Board No. 2; Beaver County Council of National Defense; local committees to regulate distribution of food and eliminate hoarding; committees to regulate and save coal, gas, light, and heat; adult committees of Minute Men; Boy Scouts; and the Chamber of Commerce as a coordinating agency.

The first memorial service for veterans in Beaver Falls was held on Sunday, November 11, 1923, at the Regent Theatre. Frank A. (Bridgie) Weber instituted this event, which is held on the Sunday before Armistice Day, which is now known as Veteran's Day.

The greatest conflict in the history of civilization, forever changing the course of history and affecting all mankind, was World War II. Even now, the images of this war remain vivid: the cowardly, treacherous attack on Pearl Harbor; the flag raising on Iwo Jima; the deadly, hot, steamy jungles of the Pacific; the awesome tank battles of Africa; and the invasion of Normandy. Once again, the men of Beaver Falls were involved in all of them.

The vast complexity and range of military action in World War II makes a complete treatment of events impossible. However, an attempt to trace the history of the 110th Infantry as a typical unit with local background, and an apology for the inability to cover other far-flung branches of our armed forces, is made.

Returning to the 110th Regiment after World War I, Colonel Edward Martin was placed in command on October 16, 1919. Colonel John Aiken later succeeded him. In 1936, the regiment was mobilized in the flood areas of Johnstown and Pittsburgh to keep order and prevent looting. By 1939, the world situation had worsened and the regiment participated in extensive maneuvers at Manassas, Virginia and in upper New York state. On February 17, 1941, it was called into service. Further, more advanced maneuvers were staged in Virginia, the Carolinas, and Louisiana. Practice in modern amphibious training was then continued in Florida and Virginia.

The regiment sailed for Europe on October 7, 1943, and landed 11 days later at Bristol, England. It practiced invasion-landing techniques for several months, and then landed on Normandy Beach, France on July 22, 1944. This was several weeks after D-Day. It engaged the enemy first on July 22, 1944, moved to Paris, and marched in the "parade" through the liberated city. The regiment then continued northeast into Belgium and Luxembourg, where it engaged in heavy fighting, ending in the capture of Hurtgen Forest. By December, the 28th Division, of which the 110th Regiment was a unit, and the 101st Airborne Division were generally credited with checking that last mighty German offensive at the close of the month.

The 110th Regiment was the first unit of the 28th Division to reach the Rhine River on February 8, 1945. It later proceeded to the German homeland by rail and motor, traveling through Belgium and the Netherlands. Following VE-Day, it occupied the Saraland for three months before returning to the United States on August 2, 1945. After a 30-day leave, the regiment assembled at Camp Shelby, Mississippi for redeployment in the Pacific Theater. Fortunately, the Japanese surrender on August 14, 1945 rendered this plan unnecessary. Consequently, the regiment was deactivated on October 25, 1945.

In Beaver Falls, Geneva College again had a military detachment on its campus during part of World War II. In contrast, this time the members were shipped from Air Force stations such as Nashville, Tennessee or Waco, Texas. Dr. M.M. Pearce, president of the college, announced that 150 Army Air Cadets would arrive on March 1, 1943. They were to be housed in Alumni Hall and in North Hall. Actually, the first 126 aviation students arrived on the Sabbath morning of February 28, at the P&LE station. Their classes were to begin on March 3, under the command of Lieutenant Howard Frazier, Lieutenant John Ward, and Lieutenant Stephen Rozakis.

The schedule called for instruction in physics, mathematics, history, English, geography, and physical education. The 36th Detachment increased to 300 students and was divided into 10 sections, each one having a leader and each one being classified by mental ability. Classes began at 7:30 in the morning, running Monday through Saturday, with many members sleepy on Monday mornings after having liberty over the weekend. Students who failed the weekly tests and the makeup test were restricted to the campus. The complete courses covered five months, but adjustments and changes were frequently made to maintain the quotas.

Dr. William E. Cleland prepared the changing master schedules, and Dr. Allen Morrell was the coordinator for President Pearce. The 36th Unit won special citation from the War Department for a public demonstration at Reeves Field on July 5, 1943. It won the rating as top college unit in Pennsylvania and placed among the top three units in colleges throughout the country. As the months passed, aviation students were no longer college students, but mostly high school graduates or promising material from the ranks. The impending close of the war in Europe resulted in the closing of the unit in the early months of 1944 and the return to the regular program at Geneva College. Excellent officers, strict discipline, and good instruction, together with sympathetic administration from the college, made the outstanding results of this program possible.

Meanwhile, on the home front, one can easily recall the blackouts, air-raid drills, rationing books, War Savings Bonds, casualty lists, censorship, and the crucial battles of the war: Guadalcanal, Midway, Normandy, Stalingrad, North Africa, Anzio, Berlin, and the atomic bombs over Japan. Teachers recall the registration of men, sugar books, gasoline stamps, and high school enlistments.

Another poignant, local memory is the funeral of A. Johnston Lewis of the Air Force, while the 36th Army Air Corps Detachment was stationed at Geneva. One can also recall the local Selective Service Board: Floyd Atwell, William Ridgeway, and Edward Jewell, and their outstanding public service. Blackouts and practice drills were conducted by another agency, the Civil Defense.

Local heroes were not always known or identified. One could include Cari Moldovan of Daugherty Township, who survived the infamous Bataan Death March in the Philippines. One can also salute Stan Namola of Chippewa, who was awarded both a Silver and a Bronze Star, together with the Purple Heart with cluster. He was described as the most decorated soldier from World War II in the Beaver Falls District. In addition to nurses in World War II, one can include WACS, WAVES, SPARS, and women in the Marines, as groups worth mentioning. Brigadier General Edward A. Sahli, one of two generals from Beaver County, compiled an outstanding record of military service. He was commanding officer of the Selective Service on the staff of Adjutant General Weber, and received a certificate of merit from General Lewis R. Hershey for his contributions.

Lieutenant General Frank (Bridgie) Weber of Beaver Falls, former Adjutant General Of Pennsylvania and one of the state's most distinguished military figures, was born in Leetsdale on April 16, 1898. He was educated in Rochester Schools, and enlisted when a youth of 19 as a Private in Machine Gun Company, 10th Infantry, Pennsylvania National Guard at Beaver Falls on June 24, 1917.

EUGENE F. JANNUZI. A native of Beaver Falls and graduate of Beaver Falls High School and Geneva College, Eugene served in World War II in the Navy. He married the former Margaret Moltrup.

G.C. MURPHY COMPANY. Located on the corner of Seventh Avenue and 11th Street, the Murphy Company arranged two fine displays to help advertise the Defense Drive during World War II.

The company was mustered into federal service in World War I on July 15 of that year, and Weber served overseas from May 23, 1918 to March 13, 1919. During action on the front lines on September 22, 1918, then a private first class, he was gassed and recovered at a base hospital in Vichy, France.

Honorably discharged March 28, 1919, upon demobilization he re-enlisted in the Machine Gun Company on February 23, 1920. Federally recognized in July of that year, the outfit became D, 110th Infantry on April 1, 1921. Subsequently, Weber was promoted to second lieutenant and then first lieutenant (Provisional). When the unit disbanded on January 25, 1924, he transferred to the National Guard Reserve.

Weber was appointed a captain of the Pennsylvania Reserve Defense Corps and assigned to Company B on May 22, 1941. In August of that year, he was appointed a major and assigned to Headquarters First Battalion, Third Infantry. In 1943, he was appointed lieutenant colonel and then colonel, being assigned to brigade headquarters. His appointment as brigadier general came April 11, 1946 and as commanding general of the Pennsylvania National Guard on May 28 of the same year.

On February 11, 1947, Weber was appointed adjutant general. In 1948, he received the rank of brigadier general and in 1949, major general. On March 6, 1952, he was appointed lieutenant general, the highest rank held by any man in the history of the Pennsylvania National Guard. His appointment as adjutant general happened on April 19, 1955.

His numerous military decorations include the Purple Heart and World War I Victory Ribbon with six battle stars, the Commendation Ribbon in World War II, the Victory Ribbon in World War II, American Defense Service Medal, American Campaign Medal, Armed Forces Reserve Medal, United Nations Service Medal, National Defense Service Medal, the Pennsylvania Distinguished Service Medal (with laurel), Pennsylvania Meritorious Medal with Laurel Leaf, Pennsylvania Service Ribbon, Pennsylvania 20-year Service Medal, National Guard World War I Medal, National Guard Victory Medal, and the Pennsylvania Distinguished Service Medal, which was awarded to him by the American Legion.

He was commander of the Beaver Falls American Legion Post 261 for 12 years and following that, served as district commander, 26th District, American Legion for four years. He was also Pennsylvania Department commander of the Military Order of the Purple Heart for one year. He organized and was the first state president of the county directors of veteran affairs.

Weber served as chairman of the Pennsylvania Aeronautic Commission, Pennsylvania Soldiers and Sailors Home, Pennsylvania Veterans Commission, Pennsylvania Civil Defense, Pennsylvania Armory Board, Pennsylvania Military Advisory Committee, and Pennsylvania Military Reservation. He was official military aide and advisor to Governors Martin, Duff, and Fine, and for six months to Governor Leader until succeeded by General Biddle.

At the end of World War II, he was in charge of paying the state's adjusted compensation. His recap is below.

Number of paid claims—veterans	1,119,331
Dollar value of paid claims—veterans	$408,302,030.00
Average amount paid per claim—veterans	$364.77
Number of paid claims—beneficiaries	38,753
Dollar value of paid claims—beneficiaries	$17,793,507.70
Average amount paid per claim—beneficiaries	$459.02

One of Weber's most tragic memories, in addition to the memory of his buddies who fell in action in World War I, happened in 1950 when the 28th Division was called into active service in the Korean War. The Division was on its way to Camp Atterbury, Indiana when a train wreck near Coshocton killed 33 guardsmen from the 109th artillery unit that was out of the Wilkes Barre area. General Weber handled arrangements in connection with the funeral. He arranged an impressive memorial service and did all in his power to assuage the grief of the families of the victims.

Our other outstanding general was the beloved Ed Sahli Sr., who earned recognition as one of the most productive, concerned, and involved leaders in the entire history of Beaver Falls. Respected not only as a businessman, religious leader, humanitarian, and civic leader, Sahli compiled a most impressive military record of leadership and organizational ability.

Ed Sahli Sr. graduated from Beaver Falls High School in 1922. An Army Reserve officer, he was called into duty during October 1941. He served for five years during World War II and was commended for his outstanding ability as the head quartermaster in charge of all supplies at Camp Aberdeen Proving Ground in Maryland.

He transferred to the National Guard in 1949 where he eventually became head of the Selective Service Division. He retired as a brigadier general on May 1, 1964. Among his many military decorations are the Army Commendation Ribbon and the Pennsylvania Distinguished Service Medal.

The Korean War was at the time the most confusing war in our nation's history. It was a war, but was never recognized as such. It was officially a police action. There were no clear winners or losers. It was a war of epic battles such as the magnificent landing at Inchon, the battle for Pork Chop Hill, the Pansum Reservoir, and countless other hills and valleys. It was the last great example of the brilliance of General Douglas MacArthur and the shock of his abrupt dismissal by President Harry Truman, concluding with the famous "old soldiers never die" speech before the joint houses of Congress.

Korea gave us the capture and eventual release of General Dean, the rise to prominence of General Mathew B. Ridgeway, and the rugged tactics of U.S. Marine General "Chesty" Puller. It also saw participation once again by many Beaver Falls soldiers.

In 1947, the 110th Infantry began annual field training at Indiantown Gap Military Reservation. By the summer of 1950, the regiment, well trained at almost authorized strength, was called into federal service and sent to Camp Atterbury, Indiana for intensive training to be followed by Exercise Southern Pines at Fort Bragg, North Carolina. The next step was troop movement of the 28th Division from Hampton Roads, Virginia to join the NATO forces in Germany. By May 1952, most of the men completed their tours of duty and returned to the United States.

Many of the local young men were individually drafted into the bitter encounter to fight and serve in all branches of the service in all locations that saw action. Most returned safely home, but some men had been prisoners of war and many died, as once again Beaver Falls's youth responded to its nation's call to arms.

No other war since the Civil War has so divided, confused, and angered our people. Every war since the War of Independence, our history has had its groups

EDWARD SAHLI SR. AND FAMILY. The Sahli family has long been active as business owners, religious leaders, and humanitarian and civic leaders.

of dissenters. This is to be expected and is inherent in man's nature. Even after the bombing of Pearl Harbor, there were thousands who still opposed our entry into World War II. But the hate and active division that tore our society apart during the Vietnam War was unprecedented.

First it was conceived as a political war, then there was never a firm declaration or policy of war established, but most importantly it was a media war covered so extensively and intimately each night on television that the public was made aware of the horror of war more convincingly than ever before. It was no longer a matter of days before information was released; quite often, live coverage would show the public their sons and daughters dying instantaneously. It became too much for many to endure.

College campus riots erupted across the nation, President Lyndon Johnson was either hailed or hung in effigy, families fought and were divided, and many young men fled to Canada to escape the draft. Jane Fonda all but destroyed her movie career for siding with the North Vietnamese and becoming known as Hanoi Jane. It was a war that left an indelible black stain upon our nation's history.

But through all the dissension and passionate rejection, Beaver Falls men once again demonstrated their patriotism by serving in large numbers in all phases of the action. Many flew helicopters; more were foot soldiers desperately fighting in

117

the swamps and jungles, while others saw the war from an aircraft cockpit or a naval vessel. When the terrible conflict ended, Beaver Falls once more earned recognition through the brave efforts of its sons and daughters.

The most recent and thankfully one of the briefest wars in American history was Operation Desert Storm. Sustained action, inaugurated by President George Bush against the state of Iraq because of aggression toward its neighboring countries, was successfully accomplished with a complete, resounding victory in less than three weeks.

Again, this was a war so totally and minutely covered by the news media that the entire world could follow the air attacks and ensuing desert action live as they actually were happening. But unlike the horror expressed with the Vietnam experience, this war was applauded and cheered by the American public. Not since the days of World War II had a military involvement been greeted with such enthusiasm.

Each war produces its outstanding generals. Vietnam had General William Westmoreland, and the Persian Gulf War gave us General H. Norman Schwarzkopf, who personified the spirit of American patriotism and fighting aggression. "Stormin' Norman" was a throwback to the days of Patton, Puller, Pershing, and MacArthur that the United States seemed to yearn for and need. He became the symbol of military pride and respect that had been missing since the days of the Korean War.

Once more, sons and daughters of Beaver Falls marched forward to serve on distant foreign soil to protect our freedom and the spread of tyranny. It is estimated that at least 18 local service people saw duty either in the air flying the precision bombing runs, at sea during the naval bombardment, or on the hot, scorching dry desert sands during this brief but violent victory.

Hopefully, there will be no more wars, but unfortunately, judging from history, this is a forlorn hope. It is in man's basic nature to be aggressive and war will always loom as the final arbitrator to disagreements. Therefore, it is sadly certain that sometime in the future Beaver Falls men and women will be called upon to answer the challenge of duty. But viewing our proud devotion, dedication, and participation from the days of the Revolution to the present, there can be no doubt that on the deadliest front lines of battle, a Beaver Falls soldier will be found.

7. Joe Namath

He has become a legend. His name is spoken in the same grouping of sports immortals as DiMaggio, Ruth, and Williams; Louis and Mohammed Ali; Jim Thorpe and Red Grange. When he dies, it will be front-page news in every newspaper in the nation.

He is Joe Namath, "Broadway Joe," and "Super Joe," football's first true superstar. Oh, there were the Bronco Nagurskis, Lou "The Toe" Groza, "Big Daddy" Lipscombe, "Crazylegs" Heirsh, and many others. But Namath was young, with an animal magnetism that made him sexually appealing and more of an entertainment personality than the standard professional football player.

He was the first to receive a truly large financial contract; he was cocky, confident, and poised, and he possessed enormous charisma. He wore colorful clothes, maintained a fabulous apartment, and dated movie stars. He boasted publicly he would deliver a Super Bowl championship and then did it. He was a super presence and he was a Beaver Falls boy.

There have been numerous other professional football players from Beaver Falls who were outstanding, and many athletes in other sports who became professionals. But there is a vast difference between a professional and a legend.

An empty football stadium is one of the loneliest places on earth. The wind whips along the silent bleachers, across the barren playing field, whistling its lonely sound, stirring up forgotten ghosts from the past. From the Reeves Stadium press box on a cold winter day, one can easily visualize the former deeds of greatness that occurred upon the gridiron, remembering the excited roar of the crowd. It's been many years since that magic season when a promise of future greatness first appeared on this field, notifying the local fans that something special had arrived. But it seems like only yesterday.

The name of Reeves Stadium, nestled on the tiny campus of Geneva College, wouldn't mean much to the average football fan until he or she realized that the college is in the city of Beaver Falls, Pennsylvania. Then, just maybe, a number of the better-informed might hear something click in their subconscious, faintly remembering that Broadway Joe Namath came from that community, and perhaps they'd begin showing a little more interest. They should, really, for Reeves Stadium has had more than its share of outstanding players stride upon its turf and go on to national fame and glory. Namath wasn't the only future professional to play there, but he was certainly one of the best.

Thus it was that on this college playing field, which is also used by Beaver Falls High School for its home games, Joe Willie Namath would first make his spectacular appearance before highly critical hometown fans and electrify the sports world of western Pennsylvania. It was Joe's senior year of 1960 when he quarterbacked his team to its section title and gave the area fans a season that is still recalled with pride and awe, as he alerted the experts that a new future star had exploded onto the scene.

If ever a young man was born to play football, it was Joe Namath. He was raised in an area that is known for its dedication to sports. His father immigrated from Hungary and worked 51 years in the hot steel mills, raising his family of four sons and hoping for a better life for them. Joe was the fourth and youngest son in a family of fine athletes. His second brother Bob was the junior high quarterback when Joe was only a youngster, and he spent many hours teaching his kid brother how to properly grip and throw a football. The future great spent countless long hours of his youth patiently throwing a ball through an old tire hung from a tree branch in the backyard of his home, perfecting his accuracy and timing. By the time he hit junior high school, Joe Willie showed a poise and confidence

REEVES STADIUM. Located at Geneva College, College Hill, this stadium is used quite often even for high school home football games.

in himself that went far beyond his years. He could already throw like a high school player.

Joe was born into a city that is typical of the sports-crazy atmosphere of western Pennsylvania. Beaver Falls is famous for its ardor for athletes from every sport. From his earliest age, Joe was surrounded by sports and steeped in sports lore from fanatical followers who resided in the city and impressed upon him the many opportunities to be gained in life through professional sports. There isn't much to do in the area for recreation except to become involved in sports. Although equally at home on a baseball diamond—Namath later received a number of contract offers from major league scouts—Joe had long ago decided a career in football would be his goal in life. It was his first and only love. Upon entering high school, Joe Willie got one of the first of many important breaks in his career when he came under the wing and guidance of coach Larry Bruno.

Bruno was born in nearby East Liverpool, Ohio and attended college at Geneva in Beaver Falls. A hustling, rugged 5-foot, 10-inch, 170-pound halfback, he was all-state in 1947 and had a brilliant playing record. Immediately after college, he was drafted by the Pittsburgh Steelers, but decided instead to take a coaching position at nearby Monaca. He stayed 11 years, amassing a fine record until 1959, when he came to Beaver Falls. It was a fateful move that would decisively affect the life of a young, skinny junior by the name of Joe Namath.

The fortunes of the Beaver Falls Tigers were not going well when Bruno arrived on the scene. The team had a number of losing seasons and the loyal supporting fans were becoming disgruntled. High school football is big business in the steel mining communities of the Beaver Valley and the residents take their local teams very seriously. Coach Bruno had inherited a losing team with bad habits that he immediately tried to correct. There was little he could do to avoid a losing season in 1959, but he was building for the future and his trained eye had already noticed the unusual ability demonstrated by his junior quarterback. His football savvy was highly stimulated by the boy's obvious skill and fluid method of hiding the ball. He even started him in one game to give him a little experience and see how he managed under pressure. The results were more than satisfactory and Larry knew he could build his attack around the boy for the following season. The coach said little during the off months, but smiled suspiciously to old friends and advised them to keep an eye open for a kid named Namath. Bruno was one of the very first to realize what he had found.

During summer practice sessions, the coach could hardly contain himself as he watched, with unconcealed wonder, the magnificent ball control displayed by his young star. He knew he had come across one of those once-in-a-lifetime players a coach always dreams of having on a team. The only flaw he detected in Namath's delivery was that the youth was taking a slight false step on the snap from center. He soon corrected this problem. The season was ready and Bruno was set to unleash his Tigers before an unsuspecting public.

What a season it was! To this day, local fans still recall the fabulous season and the pride they felt in their team, as the Tigers went all the way with an undefeated year, winning the WPIAL Class AA Section Title. There were many outstanding stars who would appear as if from nowhere that season to execute brilliant plays in their quest for victory. However, standing head and shoulders above them all, dominating the team with his presence, was the quarterback: Joe Willie Namath. He put it all together in his first full season of play, showing the fans a promise of what the future would bring. Like an uncanny field general, he dominated every game with his knowledge of ball handling and his ability, evident even then, to pick the opposition's defense to pieces. His judgment and authority were so mature, it was like watching a senior college star playing with the high school boys.

Let's take a look back in time at that season of 1960 and the unbelievable statistics compiled by Namath. Beaver Falls fans were treated to a spectacle which would never again be seen by future crowds, for unknown at that time, they were privileged to see Namath before serious college injuries hampered his great running abilities. They were treated to the sight of an almost perfect quarterback, one who could run and pass with equal prowess. As one local sportswriter described Joe that year, "he was an unmatched wizard of the gridiron, defying description with his superb, deft, ball manipulations." That year, Joe established himself as the standard by which to judge all future hopefuls. The ecstatic crowds were thrilled at the sight of this previously unknown athlete who was filled with such natural leadership.

The winning season got off to an auspicious beginning with a 43 to 13 rout over nearby Midland. The confident quarterback gave an early indication of things to come on the second play of the game. The Tigers received the ball and gained two yards on the first play of the down. Namath had detected a small opening on the left side of the line, so he faked a boot and ran through the hole, scampering a long 60 yards for a touchdown. Less than two minutes into the game, the Tigers led 7 to 0 after the conversion. And this was only the beginning! Later in the second quarter, Namath flashed through the scrimmage, picking up 5 yards and another touchdown. When the game ended, Joe Willie had astounded the fans by running 106 yards, passing for 174, and completing 10 for 18 passes, rating him at 55.5 percent completion. Two scoring passes were included.

The following week, disbelieving fans were treated to yet another shellacking of an archenemy to assure them that the previous week had not been a fluke. In fact, it was an even more impressive win, as the team shattered long-time foe New Castle 39 to 0. Until the 1960 season, the Tigers were only 3-16-3 against the powerful Lawrence County squad, and had not scored against them since 1939. Joe Willie limped into that encounter with a badly twisted ankle, but he still managed to complete 9 out of 13 passes for a fantastic 88.9 percent. Included in those stats were two touchdown bombs to his favorite receiver, young halfback Tom Krzemienski. The speedy young Krzemienski basked in the glory of that year along with his friend Joe, and then went on to a measure of fame himself. Krzemienski went to Michigan State, where he played outstanding ball. Along with Namath, he then had a brief trial with the New York Jets. In those days, a

FOOTBALL TEAM OF 1960. Joe Namath is number 19, seated beside Coach Larry Bruno. Abbie Walton is seated in the third row to the left on the end.

large number of hometown fans dreamed of seeing Namath and Krzemienski continue their brilliant high school play together as pros, but that was not to be. The Jets dropped Krzemienski and he went on to the Hartford Charter Oaks before retiring to marry and assume a teaching career. Like others on this team of destiny, he would be touched momentarily and carried along by the greatness of Namath before fading into a more normal life.

By now, Beaver Valley fans were flocking to Reeves Stadium and packing the other high school playing fields whenever the Tigers played, as word of this fantastic player had quickly spread. Football is a way of life to these hard, rugged steelworkers and their families, and they cautiously reserve their praise until the judgment is in on the athlete. In this case, there was no doubt. Namath was quickly established as one of the local greats and the faithful of Beaver Falls had quite a number of past heroes by which to evaluate him. The town had produced Joe "Tiger" Walton, the great end for the Pittsburgh Panthers, New York Giants, and the Washington Redskins. Jim "Bucky" Mutshcheller came from Beaver Falls and went on to play for Notre Dame and the Baltimore Colts. Geneva College gave us the great Cal Hubbard, a legend who played during the mid-1920s and was named to the Pro Football Hall of Fame, the College Football Hall of Fame, and incredibly, the Baseball Hall of Fame. Other local stars included Babe Parilli, Mike Ditka, Mike Lucci, Po James, and Tony Dorsett. Beaver County turned out over 40 professional football players alone, in addition to many other pro sports

BEAVER FALLS HIGH. The school Joe Namath graduated from is now the Beaver Falls Middle School on Eighth Avenue.

stars such as Richie Allan, George "Doc" Medich, and Tito and Terry Francoma in baseball; and Norm Van Lier and Pistol Pete Maravich in basketball. So, Namath was certainly in good company. It's not an idle boast when a western Pennsylvania fan claims his area is the bedrock of high school football.

The Tigers continued to roll behind the strong arm of Joe Willie. Victory number four resulted from a 25 to 13 defeat of Ambridge. Joe had a –3 rushing, passed for 85 yards, was 3 for 15 for a 20 percent average, and again connected to Krzemienski for a scoring bombshell. If the statistics seem rather poor, it becomes understandable when one learns that Namath played this game with a shoulder separation.

Victory number five came at the expense of Butler, 26 to 6. Namath's shoulder was still bothering him, but he managed to register 7 yards running, 127 passing, and complete 12 for 19 for a 68.45 percent average. His buddy Krzemienski caught two more scoring passes. By the sixth game, Namath was feeling much better physically, and responded with 17 yards running, 14 for 20 completions for a 70 percent average, and 155 total yards passing as Beaver Falls ripped Farrell 33 to 18. Russ Kerstetter, who would one day be a star player for Princeton, caught Namath's only touchdown pass during that contest. Kerstetter, along with Krzemienski, had an outstanding high school year that season.

But area fans hadn't seen anything yet, as Joe really set them hollering in the Aliquippa game, when the self-assured athlete passed for an unbelievable 248 yards. The snarling Tigers slaughtered the Aliquippa squad 34 to 7, as Namath shone at his brightest. The high yardage resulted from 13 out of 18 completions for 70.2 percent, but Namath also ran for 20 yards. Krzemienski pulled in two long, scoring aerials, and another toss went to Bo Hayden. An aura of mystery surrounds the talented figure of the fleet Bo Hayden. He was only a junior during this season, but managed to lead the entire Beaver Valley in scoring. A brilliant future seemed assured, but the next year, the quiet youth played in only two games and then dropped out of football, never to play again. However, his was one of the brightest lights to shine for this high school team of destiny before he faded away from the sports scene.

Elwood City stadium was jammed to capacity by rabid fans as the Tigers trotted onto the field for their eighth game of the year and last league encounter. It was a big one, for a win would give Beaver Falls its first section title in 32 years. Not since 1928 had the Tigers won the laurels, and they were determined to grab the crown. Again Namath dominated the action with his pinpoint accuracy and field leadership. There was never any serious doubt as to the outcome as the orange and black scampered to a 26 to 0 shutout. Joe Willie raced for 9 yards, had 12 for 21 completions for a percentage of 57.1, and accumulated a total of 224 passing yards. He threw one scoring pass to end Butch Ryan, who would be converted to quarterback the following season and lead the Tigers to another undefeated season. Later he went on to the University of Iowa and played ball before eventually returning to Beaver Falls to become an assistant coach under Larry Bruno.

The final game of the marvelous season was a non-league meeting against archrival New Brighton. The New Brighton Lions hailed from the city directly across the Beaver River and dearly wanted to spoil the Tigers's perfect record. The natural rivalry had built up over the years to epic proportions. But it was destined to be only a dream for New Brighton as Namath led the gleeful Tigers to a staggering 40 to 6 annihilation over the Lions. Joe Namath ended his high school career in a blaze of glory as he ran for 37 yards, had 10 for 17 completions for 58.8 percent, and passed for a total of 185 yards. It was a season to be long remembered.

Namath's final overall statistics for his senior were very impressive and had scouts from college campuses throughout the nation knocking on his door. The tall, skinny youth had run for a total of 275 yards and had passed for the astounding total of 1,543 yards, including 12 touchdowns. But you couldn't put down on paper the abstracts that made him so great even then at this early stage of his career. The impressive mature leadership, the ball handling and deft manipulation, and the skill with which he picked apart the opposing line. It all started back in that breathtaking senior year with the intangible qualities that would propel him to the highest peak of future professional glory. Namath entered the spotlight that season and has never left its glare to this day.

In the future lay national recognition under the colorful coaching of Paul "Bear" Bryant at Alabama, the tragic injuries to his legs, and the unforgettable glory-filled years with the New York Jets, crowned with the Super Bowl victory against the Baltimore Colts. Even movies and a show business career would beckon, but that was still to come. It all began at Reeves Stadium for Beaver Falls fans, the stadium that has witnessed so many great football figures. They had seen him in his physical excellence at the very peak of his all-around abilities. The skill he displayed and the magnetic image he projected would forever remain etched upon their memories. The years ahead would be filled with more records and glory for Joseph William Namath, but in retrospect, it's doubtful if any season gave him as much personal satisfaction or was as important to his development as his first full year under coach Bruno at Beaver Falls High School.

BEAVER FALLS BAND. In this picture, the Beaver Falls High School Marching Band is holding a concert in the old auditorium at the Carnegie Free Library. Joe would have attended many concerts here.

8. Motor Cars, Ambulances, and Santa Claus

The story of the automobile in Beaver Falls began shortly after 1900. In contrast to the 8,000 motorcars in the entire United States, Beaver County boasted a total registration of 22 autos in 1902. The local motorist of the era was a hardy soul.

Consider the experience of Frank P. Musser, the first person to drive an auto on the streets of Beaver Falls. Musser lived at 800 Seventh Avenue and was able to go down Seventh Avenue hill, but could not go up in his car. In order to drive home, he had to return via Third Avenue to 11th Street and Seventh Avenue. He would then drive down to Eighth Street. Even using this detour, he sometimes would have to get a push up to Seventh Avenue on 11th Street. History does not record the name of the vehicle driven by Musser, but it was one of the 2,200 different makes of cars manufactured in the United States since 1893.

Beaver Falls has been an outlet for many makes of cars. Many are still sold, such as Buick, Cadillac, Ford, Chevrolet, Dodge, and Oldsmobile. However, some of the cars sold in Beaver Falls at one time no longer are in production. The list would include Briscoe, Chalmers, Columbia, Dort, Fort, Franklin, Hudson, Maxwell, Rickenbacker, Stevens, Studebaker, Stutz, White Steamer, Peerless, EMF, Chandler, Reo, Flanders, and Willy Knight.

The first purchasers of autos in Beaver Falls were doctors and businessmen. Their names are well remembered by local old-timers. Drs. J.S. Louthan and H. McCreary had Buicks; Dr. E.S. Burns, an Oldsmobile; and Dr. Simpson used a Dodge coupe for house calls and a Cadillac touring car for Sunday drives. Other well-known motorists of the period were the Fair brothers, Barney and Claude; William, Steve, and Tom Moltrup; Louis Ingram, who drove an air-cooled Franklin; World War I hero Colonel Joseph Thompson, who owned a Lincoln; and Sam Creese, a Flanders.

Auto racing came almost as early as the automobile to Beaver Falls. In 1908, during Old Home Week, marking the 40th Anniversary of Beaver Falls, a race was held between two local pioneer auto dealers.

Barney O. Flair was in a two-cylinder, 14-horsepower Maxwell and Howard A. McCreary was driving a four-cylinder, Model 10 Buick. The race course began at the City Building on 11th Street (where the Union National Bank is today), to Steffin Hill, and on to Patterson Heights, down the hill, and back to 11th Street for a total distance of 5 miles. The racers were required to cover the course five times for a total distance of 25 miles.

Fair was given a 5-minute head start since he was driving a two-cylinder machine against the four-cylinder car of McCreary. McCreary still won the race by 7 minutes in a time of 1 hour, 9 minutes. He was roaring around the course at something less than 25 miles per hour. This race was the crowning event of the week and a milestone in local auto history.

A contribution of national importance was made in 1906 by a local firm, the Ingram-Richardson Manufacturing Company, when it produced the first enameled license plates. These were used by Pennsylvania and other states in the years before World War I. Before Ingram-Richardson's innovation, a motorist made his own license plate using leather and tin numbers.

Autos in the good old days came in a wide range of body types such as the touring car, phaeton, runabout, and landaulet. A prospective Buick owner could place an order for the car of his choice at the 17th Street shop of James F. McCreary, and it would be assembled there according to his wishes. Closed cars were rare. J. Bert Rimbey sold the first Chevrolet sedan to John S. Tress. The first Fords were sold by Lisle T. Miller.

Obtaining fuel was a problem for the early motorist. L.S. Lutton installed the first gas pump at his livery stable on 714/718 11th Street. The first true service station was Silk Service on Sixth Avenue.

Edward J. Spratt Sr. had the distinction of designing, constructing, and supervising the first motor driven ambulance in Pennsylvania. The ambulance was constructed in Beaver Falls in 1912 when a four-cylinder Maxwell was purchased at the B.O. Fair Garage.

Building an ambulance out of the bulky Maxwell was no easy task. The bolts on the body had to be cut. The Maxwell, which had a 114-inch wheelbase, was sawed in half. The drive shaft was disconnected and the old Keystone Driller Company made a new one. The chassis was lengthened to 134 inches. Then a local cabinetmaker built a body of wood, which was mounted on the chassis.

Spratt rented a garage between 13th and 14th Streets in back of the Montgomery Ward building, where the work was completed.

After the body was assembled another problem arose—painting. Finally, a painter from Monaca was contacted and he agreed to paint the converted Maxwell. To add the finishing touches, Spratt installed electric lights on the sides of the ambulance, oil lamps on the dash, and gas lamps for headlights—the epitome of American ingenuity back in 1912.

Despite all the bugs that had to be ironed out in actual construction of the ambulance, Spratt still contends that the hardest job of all was constructing a cot for the back. Originally, a summer cot was installed. This improvised ambulance bed was quickly abandoned after the first trip.

Mr. Spratt related that his first trip was to transport a young lady from Eighth Street in New Brighton to Providence Hospital. "My brother was inside and I was driving. Every bump I hit, I saw my brother putting the young lady back on the cot." After that first rocky ride to the hospital, Spratt had a couch specially built for the ambulance interior.

Before becoming a funeral director, Mr. Spratt was an employee of Jones and Laughlin Steel Corporation for more than six years. It was at J&L that Spratt gained much of the knowledge that he used in transforming the Maxwell into the state's first ambulance. The motorized ambulance was the rage of the city during those early years. Spratt and his marvelous machine easily braved the inclement weather to transport patients to local hospitals. It reached speeds of up to 40 miles per hour.

Although he didn't advertise the ambulance service, Spratt received more than 200 calls during 1918. The public became aware of his ingenious service by reading a story and picture that appeared in *The Daily Tribune*.

Anyone who ever ran across a local department store Santa Claus who delighted many eager-eyed children with his special kind of Christmas magic might be shocked to find out that the kindly Santa was a funeral director in the "off-season."

SPRATT AMBULANCE. This 1912 Maxwell, special four-cylinder ambulance was built at the B.O. Fair Garage. The body was built and painted by C.S. Vandling of New Brighton. The top speed was 40 miles per hour.

EDWARD SPRATT SR. Ed was married to Rose Pappert and enjoyed playing Santa Claus for over 40 years. He died in 1968 at the age of 80.

For 40 years, Edward J. Spratt Sr., long-time funeral director in the Beaver Falls-New Brighton area, also played Santa Claus. Being a mortician by profession, Spratt's occupation often called for ambulance visits to hospitals during the holiday season—and it was there that he first conceived the idea of playing Santa.

In 1916, Spratt started playing the Santa Claus role by pulling out Mrs. Spratt's sewing basket, soon creating a suit ready to be filled. And filled it had to be, for Spratt was quite slim at the time. Somehow, his wife kept visualizing how a real Santa should look and made the suit a couple sizes too large. Pillows and other stuffing came to the rescue, and it wasn't long before Spratt was off on his first journey to local hospitals.

The original suit lasted two years—then one was bought from a costume company. The delight of portraying Santa became such an obsession that Spratt actually began living the part. Authenticity was his goal, so he set about getting an outfit that would make him look like the real thing right down to the last button.

Rich velvet material was purchased, while fluffy fur was used for the trimming, and a 4-inch-wide white leather belt with a large gold buckle topped off the outfit. The new costume was ready for another holiday.

After the suit was fitted to perfection, the search began for an appropriate wig and whiskers to eliminate the discomfort of wearing a false face. A white wig came from New York and the whiskers came from a costume firm in Pittsburgh. Though the suit stood more than 20 years of wear, it is reportedly still in good condition.

Bells with just the right sound were purchased from a music company in Texas. A leather strap was ordered from Elkhart, Indiana and when both arrived, a saddler mounted the bells on a strap to be used for providing a type of reindeer-sleigh sound effect that most youngsters expect to hear.

Several years later, Spratt was presented with a pair of black patent leather boots with white kid tops, specially made by the Florsheim Company. A course in makeup enabled Spratt to supply the finishing touches to his characterization.

After many heartwarming experiences, Spratt related, "There are many tears shed in making all these visits, and this was one time when I was fit to be tied when arriving home."

Many local experiences shared a cherished spot in Spratt's long memory. Such an experience occurred on an annual Christmas Eve visit to Beaver Valley General Hospital. Though most children's requests are for toys, one little tot pushed toys out of his mind when approaching Santa. While Spratt was talking merrily to a patient, he felt that gentle tug so familiar to Saint Nick and looked down to find a small boy at his side. "Please Santa," he began, "bring me some clothes for Christmas so I can go to Sunday school. I'm wearing my sister's shoes." And there stood the little boy, with an outstretched leg, showing shoes that curled at the toes because they were too big.

Through the help of a nurse, the name of the boy (who had been visiting his sick grandmother), his age, and address were obtained. As Christmas fell on a Sunday that year, Spratt had to send his wife to a New Brighton merchant the next day, asking if he would open his store so she could buy clothing for the needy child.

Once clothing from head to foot was secured, Spratt put on his coat and hat and headed for the child's home. When arriving, his message was: "I was at the hospital last night when you were. Santa said that he was a little late, but that he wanted me to deliver these presents to you."

It was many years later that a soldier approached Spratt in his New Brighton establishment and said, "You probably don't remember me, Mr. Spratt, but I was the little boy you gave those clothes to on Christmas Day and I'll never forget your kindness."

Spratt was Santa for Beaver Valley people for three generations. With his plump figure, bushy eyebrows, hearty laugh, and that necessary twinkle in his eye, Santa was never better represented.

9. DISASTERS

It began as any other typical Friday on the last day of May 1985. Business was usual, lives were normal, and the day started out with sunny skies that turned overcast by mid-afternoon. The forecast called for the possibility of heavy showers.

But far above the Beaver Valley, unique weather conditions were forming and randomly coming together—unusual conditions that happen rarely, but when they do, often unleash the most terrible of nature's forces. Such were the conditions so rapidly forming.

Chuck Heckler, a National Weather Service meteorologist, first noted the possibility of a bad situation around 3 p.m. and began observing the developing conditions closely. By 5 p.m., there was no doubt about it any longer and the first alert that a tornado watch was in effect for western Pennsylvania and eastern Ohio was issued. A severe thunderstorm warning was broadcast at 8 p.m. for Beaver and Lawrence Counties, but by then it was only a matter of minutes before the storm touched down.

Local radio station WBVP and Pittsburgh's KDKA ran the tornado watch as the lead story on their 5 p.m. newscasts. Throughout the following hours, the bulletin was repeatedly announced, alerting all listeners. The area television stations began their bulletin about 5:30 p.m.

It was around 7 p.m. that the thunderstorm struck. Booming thunder and brilliant lightning filled the air and lit up the skies while a heavy rain pelted the area. Strong winds whistled through the city, rattling windows and bending trees. But although it was severe in its intensity, no one really considered it unusual. Most regarded it as just another thunderstorm.

Residents in Darlington, however, were noticing something quite different and unusual. As the storm abated somewhat, people sensed that a different atmosphere was now in residence.

Mr. And Mrs. William Smith of Darlington along with their daughter Darlene Tate were standing in their backyard gazing uneasily at the sky. Mr. Smith stated, "It was humid and sultry even after the shower. The sky was a very unusual color and the clouds were swirling. Part of the sky was jet black as though it were midnight, but there were tinges of greenish purple, even streaks of fiery red mingled with grays and whites. I'd never seen anything quite like it before."

EDGEWOOD ROAD. This is a shot of the damage from the tornado, looking across Edgewood Road from the Dainton home.

Darlene Tate reported, "You could actually see the two different huge cloud masses come together. There was a horrible loud clash like a cannon being shot and then it seemed like clouds were shooting everywhere."

At 8:13 p.m., the deadly funnel cloud touched earth. Smoky gray in color, it began its murderous journey just west of McKinley Road and north of 37th Street in Chippewa Township. It would finish its nightmarish trip some 80 miles and 20 minutes later. Most residents will never forget the hideous sound as the twister moved randomly across the earth.

The intimidating funnel rapidly pursued its course crushing homes and leveling trees as a child might sweep away a toy. Locally, the twister left a 13-mile path of ruin before touching down elsewhere on this deadly night. It spent only 20 minutes in the local area resulting in damage that totaled over $8 million. But most importantly on this memorable night, tornados claimed the lives of 61 people. Three local people were only seconds from death.

Nineteen minutes and seven seconds after 8 p.m., it was done, lasting only a few brief minutes. It had hit and was gone before some people had a chance to scream.

It rose over a slight wooded incline, across the B&O Railroad tracks, skidded over Route 18, and slammed into the Big Beaver Shopping Plaza, which technically is located only a few yards from the Beaver Falls city limits.

The destruction was on a gigantic scale. The roof was completely ripped off the Gerello Beverage Company and the walls collapsed, burying Frank Gerello for a number of terrifying moments until he was rescued. The roof flew through the

133

air and completely leveled a row of parked cars as effectively as a bulldozer. A semi trailer was rolled onto its side by the mammoth wind.

Strewn throughout the parking lot were pieces of metal, wood, and broken glass. All of the stores had been devastated. Light poles had snapped or were bent. The huge triangular marquee that identified the shopping plaza lay twisted on the ground. Overturned, flattened cars were everywhere, crumpled and wedged together. It seemed that an atomic blast couldn't have been more devastating.

The Big Beaver Restaurant had nearly all of its glass doors and windows blown out and the ceiling was torn away. In all, 14 buildings in the plaza were destroyed. It was a Jamesway store that was the focus of attention. The massive store with its rows of gleaming and varied merchandise was now just a broken shell of a building that saw a flurry of activity from the rapidly arriving police, fire, and rescue units.

Mary Griffith of Darlington was standing by her cash register, staring out the window at the storm when the funnel raced across the highway. Suddenly, the window blew in and she was covered by glass, rain, and debris. She automatically fell to the floor. There were 15 employees on duty and just as many customers when the disaster hit. The assistant manager grabbed the microphone and coolly kept repeating for everyone to lie down.

Since Jamesway was the largest store, it was natural that rescuers ran to it, but it was the state liquor store where death struck. Killed instantly by the collapsing

ALBERT DAINTON HOME. The remains of the back of the Dainton home, located on Edgewood Road in North Sewickley Township, after the tornado hit the area.

walls were Carl A. Masketti, who was an employee of the store and well known and respected, and Gladyce Brenson, who had been purchasing refreshments for her son Walter, visiting his hometown from Youngstown, Ohio. Brenson was a highly admired Beaver Falls decorator and seamstress, well known for her creative fashions.

In addition to the tragic deaths of Brenson and Masketti, it was learned later that a third victim, Dianne Lynn Flinner, had been killed at a lingerie party that she was hosting at the home of Mr. and Mrs. Jim Carney on Bennetts Run Road in North Sewickley Township. The house collapsed on her.

The three deaths were certainly far too many, but it could have been much worse considering the devastation. There were 10 victims admitted to the Medical Center of Beaver County with another 38 injured, treated, and released. Life Flight flew 2 North Sewickley residents to Allegheny General, while 5 were admitted and 40 treated and released at Ellwood Hospital.

The plaza was seriously wounded. It lay twisted and crumbled and would take years to recover. But the death funnel was not even finished. Even as the walls were still falling, the finger of destruction was scouring the 200-foot hill behind the shopping complex and roaring across the Beaver River, uplifting tremendous amounts of water.

After breeching the river, the cloud raced up the hillside, through the woods, and into the heavily populated North Sewickley area where, within moments, it killed Mrs. Flinner.

It leveled large sections of woodland like they were matchsticks. A tornado can have several effects on trees. Most trees fall on opposite sides of the path. But sometimes the twister plucks off only the tops of trees, and at other times it rips them completely out of the ground. Occasionally, it carries an entire tree many miles before smashing it to the earth.

When the funnel rammed into North Sewickley Township, it tore apart homes and tossed cars high into the air. Kemp's Meat Market was leveled and several nearby businesses demolished. The Spotlight 88 Drive-In Theater, which had long been a local landmark, was completely destroyed. A near fatal tragedy was averted there when young Judy Lash, a ticket seller, was hit in the head by flying planks and hovered for a day in critical condition before recovering. She was hospitalized for two months.

As many as 10 to 15 residences were leveled, 50 more were judged to be beyond repair, and another 200 were damaged. The tornado continued on its way along Route 588 toward Brush Creek Park and finally vanished from the immediate area leaving death, silence, and destruction behind.

Within moments of the fatal encounter, Beaver Falls Mayor Leo J. Hegner ordered all city departments to immediately rush to the scene to begin rescue and safety operations. Within half an hour, 19 policemen were at the scene directing traffic, setting up medical and rescue posts, sifting through the rubble, and organizing the chaos into some type of order. Technically, it was the Big Beaver jurisdiction, but on this night, no one said a word about invisible boundary lines.

City and volunteer firemen were at the scene within moments. Shortly after that, the Salvation Army arrived. Soon, countless volunteers were streaming into the devastated area along with other county and area township units. Within hours, the National Guard Company B, 28th Signal Battalion, which was stationed in Chippewa Township, was on hand.

State Representative Mike Veon was one of the first elected officials to arrive and assess the damage. Early Saturday morning, Governor Richard Thornberg, Senator James Ross, and Congressman Joe Kolter flew in by helicopter to survey the scene. Expressing his shock and sympathy, the governor quickly declared the area a disaster and ordered state funding and help.

It took several months before all the debris was finally hauled away and even in 2002, 17 years later, the scars on the hillsides remain and one can easily trace the path of the funnel. Some who experienced the storm first-hand still have nightmares. Many now panic and are excessively frightened by a severe storm and the families of the slain still grieve. It was a storm the citizens of Beaver Falls will never erase from their memory and will always fear for the future.

Strange objects often fall from the sky. Things like huge blocks of ice, fish, worms, frogs, or stones and rocks, and sometimes planes vanish from the sky for no reason and with no explanation.

Sometimes the sky can turn black in the middle of the day like it did in Beaver Valley on September 24, 1950.

It was on a Sunday and it started innocently enough. It was a pleasant, sunny morning and those on their way to church enjoyed temperatures in the mid-60s. But by the time church let out, the sky was hazy—a strange hazy that wasn't clouds or a muggy appearance.

Jim Reynolds Jr. wrote about the day:

> By early afternoon, I decided to go to the movies with my grandma. She was a great movie fan. I was only 9 years old at the time and lived over the old Regent Theater with my parents who worked at the theater. The matinee began at 2 pm and shortly before the hour, my grandma and I went downstairs and were stunned to see a yellow sky. The sky and all the clouds were pure yellow, as though a filter had been passed over it.
>
> It was more than a little frightening. We went to the show and during the course of the film, I would go into the lobby and glance outside. I grew more frightened as the yellow faded into a dull blue and then into a pitch black. A heavy, enveloping blackness that was terrifying in its suddenness. I wondered if the end of the world was upon us.
>
> The blackness was still in force when the film was over. We went upstairs to my parents' apartment where they were silent and nervous and the atmosphere was tense.
>
> Fortunately, by 5 pm, it was obvious the darkness was receding and the sickly yellow cast was again over the heavens. The next day,

everything was back to normal, but I would never again look at the sky and feel quite the same.

That day caused a lot of fear and panic on the local level. City street lights weren't turned on and cars were forced to travel at an extremely slow rate of speed. The darkness was responsible for the death of a pedestrian in Tyrone, Pennsylvania. While trying to cross a street, the pedestrian was struck by a car and killed. Because of the immense darkness, the driver never saw him.

In Pittsburgh, at old Forbes Field, the Pirate-Cincinnati double-header was being played under lights. In Erie, Pennsylvania, at an American Football League game, lights were also turned on.

Two racecar drivers at New Kensington were injured. Stores closed early as employees ran home. Bell Telephone Company reported an overload of 8,000 calls as panic-stricken residents called family and friends. Chickens and farm animals went to sleep, thinking night had fallen. Local police were swamped with calls for information. To this day, there is debate about what caused the blackness. The official story is that a vast forest fire in Canada was responsible and the blackness was only high, drifting smoke.

It was Thanksgiving weekend in 1950; the big meal had been eaten, the leftovers were being prepared for box lunches, the weekend was upon everyone, and new

SPOTLIGHT 88. The drive-in theatre never recovered. The sign says "gone with the wind" (a play on words). Spotlight 88 was located at the corner of Mercer Road and Route 588, and is now a flea market.

SEVENTH AVENUE. The big snow of 1950 finds a tractor trying to clear a path for cars down the avenue. This is the 1200 block of that street.

early Christmas ads could be seen in *The News-Tribune*. But no one would get serious about Christmas for at least another week.

All four local theaters were doing steady business; especially the Rialto, which featured one of the year's top movies, *King Solomon's Mines* with Stewart Granger and Deborah Kerr. The Regent was showing *Girl's School* and *Davy Crockett Indian Fighter* with George Montgomery. Robert Ryan was the star of *Born to be Bad*, showing at the Granada. The State Theater offered *I'll Get By*.

Friday night shoppers in Beaver Falls had a huge variety of stores to shop from with a large selection of merchandise. Morrow Motors was displaying the new 1951 Fords that in some cases cost more than $1,000. Gross Furniture was selling a four-piece furniture group for $69.50, while Bachelors featured carpeting starting at $11.95. You could purchase ice skates for $14.95 at Burkes Auto Store or a Fruit of the Loom men's white shirt at Benson's for $1.99.

If you wanted to take the family to dinner, you had your choice of Joe's Café, the Eatwell, the Sandwich Shop, Rio Grill, Little Italy, Zoe's Dining Room, Johnny's Restaurant, Beals, the Sweet Shop, and a great many others.

Local radio station WBVP, which had only been on the air for three years, had forecast cold weather with a chance of snow and a low in the upper 20s to low 30s. Therefore, no one was too surprised when it began snowing at 5 p.m. on Friday, November 24.

The snow continued to fall steadily throughout the day. It was a heavy, wet snow that began to accumulate quickly. WBVP changed its forecast late in the day and was now calling for perhaps 6 to 8 inches of the white stuff. Some people began to be mildly alarmed and some sensed this was rather unusual, but most citizens went about their business and figured it was just another snowstorm.

But it wasn't an average snowfall. It was a blizzard and the conditions came together to turn it into a monster storm that no one expected. It kept snowing without letting up—a wet, heavy, silent snow that by late Friday had turned the city to a ghostly white and began causing some severe traffic conditions. As people were preparing for bed, close to 1 foot had fallen and it showed no signs of letting up.

Saturday morning saw city residents awaken to a nightmare. It was no longer a laughing matter or just another typical snowfall. By now, 24 inches had fallen and in some places, the winds had created 8- to 10-foot drifts and it was still snowing.

Traffic was snarled and had come to a virtual stop. No cars traveled the main avenue and a Beaver Valley Transit Bus trying to make its run to Pittsburgh had become hopelessly stuck near Morado Dwellings, blocking what little traffic there was. The street department did its best to clear the main avenue, but was inadequately equipped to handle such a challenge.

Commuter trains attempted their early morning runs to Pittsburgh, but in vain. The trains were cancelled when the first took four hours to reach Pittsburgh and was unable to return.

Some brave souls tried to get to work and a few did. Many citizens were grateful that some of the local grocery stores managed to open, providing food and critically needed items along with a few drugstores and restaurants. The situation had grown dangerous.

Future news writer Kitty McGraw recalls feeling very committed to get to her job on a switchboard at the local Bell Telephone Company. "I knew the girls on duty would be understaffed and literally swamped with thousands of calls and I would be needed." Kitty remembers trying vainly to get her car to operate, but finally being forced to walk from Eighth Street in Patterson Township down Ross Hill and eventually reaching the establishment. "The snow was practically up to my knees and very heavy," Kitty reflected. "I left my home at 6:45 and never reached work until close to 9 am. The other girls were overjoyed to see me, as many had been unable to get to work. I stayed the entire weekend and we took turns working shifts and fortunately had cots to sleep on. Stores like Snowdens sent us coffee and sandwiches. It was a long unbelievable weekend."

Future Beaver Falls police chief Don Burdine remembers that work crews and equipment that were working nearby on the Pennsylvania Turnpike rushed to the city and pitched in to clear the streets and highway. "I know one thing," chuckled

Burdine, "most kids in town made more money shoveling snow that weekend than they had ever made in their lives. I was one of them."

Jim Reynolds Sr., the janitor of the Regent Theater and father of a future mayor, shoveled a pathway from the corner where Montgomery Ward was located, back to the theater, and on to the Isaly's store to provide walking for pedestrians. He did it several times during the day, each time taking more than an hour. He even opened the theater for business and unbelievably, some people actually arrived to see the movie. But by Sunday and into the next week, all theaters in the city were closed along with most of the other city businesses.

Some people didn't appreciate the danger. A Rochester man died as he struggled to walk to work while numerous area residents suffered heart attacks shoveling snow. The entire roof of the Monaca Skating Rink collapsed. Throughout Saturday, it continued to snow and by late evening, 36 inches had been recorded. Drifts of 10 to 12 feet covered some cars. The storm did not taper off until early Sunday morning.

Since the average home in 1950 did not have a television, most families huddled around the radio for news and entertainment. WBVP on Saturday evening was broadcasting *Polka Time* and *Music You Want*, along with updated weather bulletins.

KDKA was airing *People are Funny*, *Your Hit Parade*, and the *Judy Canova Show*, while WJAS featured music with Vaughn Monroe, Hopalong Cassidy, Gene Autry, and Gangbusters. On KQV, you could listen to the Pie Traynor sports show, *20 Questions*, and *Hawaii Calls*.

It was a long weekend and a frightening one for many residents who were not well stocked with food or for lonely people with no one to help them. The blizzard graphically demonstrated that the forces of nature could still dominate man at any time.

There would be more storms in the future. Another major snowstorm, oddly enough, would strike on a Thanksgiving weekend a few years after the one in 1950. There would be floods and even a tornado lurking in the future, but for most residents, the great snowstorm of 1950 is the most outstanding Beaver Falls encounter with nature.

10. A Hotbed of Activity

Knives . . . forks . . . axes . . . hoes . . . hinges . . . china . . . coal . . . steel . . . drills
. . . sewing machines . . . bicycles . . . typewriters . . . amusement park equipment
. . . bridges . . . railroad axles . . . tubes . . . organs . . . enameled iron works . . .
beer . . . whiskey . . . sashes and doors . . . soap . . . crankshafts . . . saws . . . mantels
. . . fireplace goods . . . piston rods . . . septic tanks . . . chemicals . . . stoves . . .
hollow ware . . . barrels . . . flour . . . clothing . . . cork . . . fire brick . . . ceramics
. . . tiling . . . elevator guides . . . plates for dollar bills.

Into these products can be read the history and strength of Beaver Falls for the
past 200 years. "A Very Pittsburgh in miniature" is what an 1876 historian called
it, marveling not only at its industries but at the railroads, canals, and hundreds of
businesses bred by those industries.

These sprang from hard-working resources, from transportation, and from
hard-working enterprising people—water, railroads, highways, and families like
the Reeves, the Pattersons, Hoopes, Townsends, Robertsons, Mayers, Ingrams,
Richardsons, McDanels, Moltrups, and the indomitable Harmony Society.

The flats along the river spawned industry after industry, one after another,
often one building on the ruins or remains of its predecessors. And the ruins
extend as far back as 1801 and into the present.

While the first settlers came to Beaver Falls about 1793, it wasn't until 1801 that
the first "industrialist" began operation. This was David Hoopes, who purchased
100 acres around what was known as the middle falls of Big Beaver Creek.
Appropriately, he set up a sawmill to meet the home-building needs of the people.

This was followed in 1806 with the erection of an iron forge. Shortly afterward,
however, Hoopes sold to Isaac Wilson, the operator of the Red Front, a Townsend
Company–sponsored trading post and merchandising supply house in Fallston. In
1808, Barker and Gregg joined Wilson, and the company became known as
Wilson and Company.

For the next four years, this blast furnace put out pigs, hollow ware, and store
supplies. Bad times came in 1812, however, and though Barker and Gregg bought
out Wilson, they quickly sold to Oliver Ormsby, who operated the furnace until
1818. But it was already failing. The War of 1812 and the scarcity of timber from
which charcoal for the furnace was derived, forced the closing of the business.

What happened to the industrial potential between then and 1828 and 1829 when the Pattersons and Robertsons arrived isn't documented. There were small businesses such as the fancy soap and candle business started by Isaac Warren Sr. in 1812 around Seventh Street. There were hotels and cabinetmakers, and other related service businesses.

The big boost, however, came when James Patterson, an easterner as they called him back then, secured 1,300 acres of land including exclusive rights to a dam (and the resultant power) across the river. Patterson built a flourmill, cooper shop, and cotton mill. He also surveyed and laid out the town in lots.

At about the same time, Archibald Robertson built a steam paper mill on Ninth Avenue at Fifth Street and it remained there for 20 years. It was later moved to the upper dam.

According to the Harris Business Directory, by 1841 there were 300 residents in Brighton, as Beaver Falls was originally known. Patterson's flourmill employed 6 and put out 200 barrels of flour a day. His cooper shop required 16 employees, and his cotton mill was operated by 35 men and had a production of 3,000 pounds of yarn a week.

The Robertson paper mill had four steam engines and an unidentified staining establishment gave employment to ten families. A list of those employed in the town indicates that in addition to the flourmill, cooperage, cotton mill, and paper mills there were the following trades:

Maid, innkeeper, blacksmith, farmer, engineer, carpenter, clerk, coal digger, machinist, canal boat captain, tanner, sign painter, cabinet maker, forge man, brick maker, merchant, shoemaker, wheat agent, soap maker, saddler, and wagon builder.

By 1853, James Patterson was ready to dispose of his businesses and he found three easterners who were willing buyers. Apparently, much was expected of them, but things went from bad to worse. An arsonist burned down the cotton mill and "the panic" in 1857 did the rest. As one writer put it, "After a sickly existence under unwise management, the company utterly failed." Patterson, who held the mortgage, foreclosed and the Harmony Society in turn foreclosed on Patterson. The property was sold at a sheriff's sale and in 1859, the Harmony Society obtained possession.

Out of these ashes grew many small industries in the following 10 or 15 years including potteries, stoneware, and the like. But by 1867 and 1868, another larger "central" industry—The Beaver Falls Cutlery Company—was in operation. This, like many other enterprises of the second half of the nineteenth century, was a Harmony Society project and it employed 300 people. It closed in 1886.

What the river and its natural resources and the canal did for the first half of the century, the railroads did for the second half. By 1876, there were 70 trains a day running through the community and the activity spawned many industries. The following list comes from 1904:

Tenth Street Bridge. This recent photograph was taken from the New Brighton side of the Beaver River. You can see the rear view of the buildings of Mayer China in lower Beaver Falls. (Photographer, Paul Couderc.)

The Beaver Falls Steel Works, Abel Peddar & Company, began in 1875 with a capacity of 1,400 tons per year of crucible cast steel.

Pittsburgh Hinge Company, hinge and chain manufacturer started in 1870, later became Pittsburgh Chain Company (burned on October 25, 1885) and Baker Chain & Wagon Iron Company.

The Mayer China Company, founded in 1881

The Union Drawn Steel Company

Keystone Driller Company, founded in 1882

Western File Limited, largest of its kind in the world making 2,400,000 files in 1876

Joseph Graff Company Axe & Hoe Works, came to Beaver Falls in 1871 from Pittsburgh

Beaver Falls Co-operative Foundry Works, founded in 1872 on the west side of town, produced stoves, hollow ware, etc.

Emerson, Ford & Company Saw Works, founded in 1871 with sales from Maine to Texas and even New Zealand

Economy Stove and Hollow Ware Works, founded in 1868—in 1875 it manufactured 4,520 cooking and heating stoves and 17,360 pieces of hollow ware

H.M. Meyers & Company Ltd Shovel Works

Beaver Falls Flour Mills "rebuilt lately" in 1904

Wilson and Brierly and Simon Harold & Company, both planning mills

Burial Casket Works

Beaver Falls Machine Shop

Beaver Falls Foundry

Hall Brothers Carriage Shop

Many brick and glass plants and a paper mill

Some of those who came and went prior to 1905 included:

J.H. Knott & Company, a flouring mill founded in 1882 on the site of the old Patterson mill, which burned down the year before, sold in 1896

Cooperative Foundry Association

HOWARD STOVE COMPANY. Founded in 1868, the company continued to operate until 1940. Howard Stoves were shipped all over the world.

Keystone Chemical Company, founded in 1887, manufactured silicate of soda in the rear of Mayer Company

Hartman Steel Company, founded in 1883, employed 900 men, bought in 1892 by Carnegie Phipps & Company; 1895, Carnegie Steel Company; 1895, Consolidated

Steel & Wire Company; 1898, American Steel & Wire Company of Illinois;1899, American Steel & Wire Company of New Jersey, shut down in 1899 and absorbed by U.S. Steel Company in 1901

Metric Metal Works, made gas meters from 1888–1892, moved to Erie

Eclipse Bicycle Company, founded in 1892 and moved in 1896

McCool Tube, founded in 1896, absorbed in 1901 by Shelby Tube Company

Beaver Falls Iron Company, founded in 1885, burned down in 1888

Beaver Falls Car Works, founded in 1878, burned down in 1886, later became General Machinist Company, went out of business in 1897

Penn Bridge Company, moved to Beaver Falls in 1878, originally known as T.B. White & Sons Bridge Works, burned down in 1907 and rebuilt on College Hill where East Works of B&W are now

Beaver Falls Iron Company, founded in 1875, burned in 1881 and rebuilt in 1893, absorbed by the Crucible Steel Company of America in 1900

The Howard Stove Company, founded in 1868, burned twice, sold in 1883, was reorganized after Al F. Wolfe sold to J.D. Perrot, Gawn Ward, and Jacob Eckie and continued in operation until 1940

Beaver Falls Flouring Mill, rebuilt in 1882, formerly James Patterson's mill, then became the John H. Knot Company

Wilson & Brierely Mill, located on the race (Fifth Street & First Avenue), became E&B Casket Company & burned down

Simon Harold & Company, founded in 1886, later became the Beaver Falls Planing Mill

The Beaver Valley Trunk Company, founded in 1893, operated until 1897

Walker & Hillman's Brush Works on Fifth Street & Walnut Run, became the plow factory of Brown Manufacturing Company

Long gone but certainly not forgotten is the Beaver Falls Cutlery Company, makers of "Table and Pocket Cutlery." This was one of the many business enterprises of the Harmony Society, or Economites, as they were known when they settled in their final home in Old Economy in Ambridge, Pennsylvania. There was a cutlery in Rochester in 1866, operating under the name of Binns & Mason making pocketknives. In 1867, the Harmony Society brought that cutlery to Beaver Falls and expanded the business to include tableware forks, knives, and kitchen knives, as well as pocketknives. The pieces were useful and durable, and many are still around and valued as collector's items.

A good selection of the items are on display at the Beaver Falls Historical Museum, including a certificate for 50 shares of stock in the company issued July 10, 1872 at a price per share of $100 to Joseph W. Knott, a bookkeeper at the cutlery, by Jacob Henrici, President Pro Tem.

Along with the stock certificate is a set of ivory-handled knives that belonged to Mr. Knott, who joined the company in 1870 at the age of 26 and was employed there until 1884. Mrs. Andrew Lester donated the knives to the museum. They are quite attractive with long, broad blades and ivory handles, some with carvings, some with metal inlays.

Another set of tableware in the display consists of three-tined forks and ivory-handled knives. These were donated by Martha Hotlzmann and came from the estate of her grandmother, Mrs. Magdalena Holtzmann. Part of the beauty of the knives lies in the etching of the company trademark on the blades, which depicts an American Eagle flapping its wings in triumph over the British Lion.

Also in the display at the museum is a pearl-handled knife donated by Miss Alice Clayton, who says the pearl handles were fashioned by her grandfather; a large kitchen knife with a wooden handle donated by Mrs. H.E. Hodgetts; several folding pocketknives; and photos of some of the Chinese workers who were employed at the cutlery.

Dr. C.G. Hussey, General Thomas M. Howe, and James W. Brown of Pittsburgh organized the Beaver Falls Cutlery Company in 1867. Brown was later a member of Congress from Allegheny County and also president of the Colonial Steel Company of Monaca. A charter was obtained on October 13, 1867 and the plant was started on a small scale in Rochester, Pennsylvania, but was soon moved to Beaver Falls where operations began in 1868 on the extensive premises in the lower end of town, familiarly known as "the cutlery property." In 1870, the concern was changed to a joint-stock company, the ownership passing largely into the hands of the Harmony Society. The capital stock of the company was $400,000 and during the height of its prosperity, its plant turned out over 14,400 finished cutlery products.

Existing sketches show that the cutlery buildings were really quite extensive. There were four or five of them, some two stories high and one building three stories high. They were located about where the approach to the Beaver Falls end of the Beaver Falls–New Brighton Bridge is now.

The Beaver Countian, a publication of the Resource and Research Center for Beaver County and Local History in the Carnegie Free Library, tells this story about the cutlery:

> As their industries increased, the Harmony Society had to hire outside people. In 1872, Englishmen from cutleries in Sheffield, England were working in the Economy-owned cutlery. Things were going very well, so this was the feasible time for a strike for higher wages. Acting as the Society's agent, John Reeves brought Chinese from California and New Orleans to break the strike. The Chinese seemed a threat not only to the

workers, but also to the saloonkeepers who knew Chinese did not drink. The arrival of the Chinese posed a problem in Beaver Falls. A town meeting was held and a delegation went to the Society with their grievances. The solution was, all cutlery workers were paid each month with the privilege of leaving if dissatisfied and if they would leave the Chinese alone and permit them to remain, the strikers would be reinstated with pay and all profits from the cutlery would be used for the community for seven years. The workers settled their dispute.

There was quite a curiosity in town to see the Chinese at work and visitors came from Ohio and Pittsburgh just to look. In one day, about $600,000 worth of goods were sold from the factory sample room, which was a lot of money at that time.

The first cutlery works that manufactured pocketknives was Binns & Mason in 1866 located in Rochester, Pennsylvania. It was merged with the cutlery works and named the Beaver Falls Cutlery Company, owned by the Harmony Society. Henry T. Reeves became the president and John Reeves was named secretary and treasurer. The building occupied a tract of land under a roof of more than 100,000 square feet of floor space and between 1 and 2 acres of ground. At times, 300 people were employed.

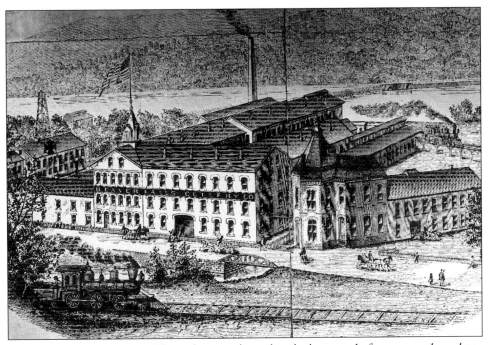

BEAVER FALLS CUTLERY. The cutlery was located at the lower end of town, was brought to Beaver Falls in 1867, closed in 1886, and employed over 300 people. The building was later used by various industries.

It is thought that it was the suggestion of the Methodist Protestant minister, the Reverend Dyer, to bring the Chinese here because Reverend Dyer was actively interested in Chinese mission work and familiar with the adaptability of the race. In turn, he was going to teach then Christianity and give them religious instruction.

John Reeves set out for California, which certainly was not a pleasure trip in those days. It took him 15 days to reach San Francisco. Reeves made several contacts, but the Chinese were reluctant to leave California on such a faraway venture. Reeves learned that there were several Chinese working in Louisiana on a new railroad line and that the work was coming to an end. He was successful in talking them into coming further east to take up new employment. Reeves was soon homeward bound with 70 of the workers and another 30 followed the next Sunday evening, July 1, 1872. They were to be met by Henry Reeves and the Reverend Dyer, but as word spread, a large group of people including the striking workmen gathered and vowed vengeance. The whole police force of the town included one constable, James C. Crane, and with the arrival of the train, the party fell back and was silent. However, it was necessary for John Reeves and Judge Henry Hice, counsel for the Harmony Society, to remain at the factory for several weeks to maintain order. Later on, more Chinese arrived and at one time, there were approximately 225 working at the cutlery. These men were all housed at the Mansion House, located on the lower end of Seventh Avenue. There was a cookhouse, dining room, and sleeping quarters. A block of wood was used for a pillow.

The contract to furnish the Chinese labor was made with Ah Chuck, a San Francisco merchant. The men were paid $1 a day in gold and the company was to keep them supplied with rice and living quarters. No time was lost because of drunkenness, but some was lost because of the use of opium. It was not as much as the time lost to the use of liquor among the white men.

During their five-year stay, the Chinese were peaceable, industrious, and order-loving men, never known to insult a woman on the street and courteous to all. The white people annoyed the Chinese by pushing them off the wood walkways into the mud street. Ah Chuck was here only at intervals, but he did leave an interpreter who was responsible to the company for the conduct of the men. He was also responsible to his government for the safe return of the Chinese remains to their native country if they should die while they were here.

Lee Ten Pay, a nephew of Ah Chuck, was the first interpreter and he spoke English with ease. Later on, Chow Hung came and brought his wife with him, who was the only Chinese woman in Beaver Falls. She stayed in her apartment and was rarely seen in public, but the women of the town did call upon her and found her very friendly.

They adhered closely to their own habits and manners of living. Many of them started to take an interest in the local entertainment and events that were held at the Presbyterian Church. It wasn't long until various churches established missions for them, but the Presbyterians were the first to open their doors so they could attend an afternoon Sunday school.

An advertising folder printed by the cutlery tells an interesting story:

> At the Centennial in Philadelphia in 1876 was exhibited the largest knife and fork in the world, manufactured by the Beaver Falls Cutlery Company. This knife is one-third larger than one made in Sheffield last year on the occasion of the Prince of Wales' visit to that place. It was the largest knife made up to that time. The entire knife is nine feet, seven inches long with a blade width of 10 inches. The knife and fork cost $1,500 and the handles were made of solid ivory, each one using an entire elephant's tusk. Their handles are beautifully carved with flowers and vines. The set was made in true proportion to the ordinary articles in an 8 to 1 scale. Thus it would require a man who was 9 feet square and 48 feet high to gracefully manipulate the steel.
>
> Suppose a man was the average height of five feet, eight inches and well built, the following are the mathematical dimensions as worked out upon that basis, of the "he" who could handle the knife and fork referred to above: head, 15 feet, four inches around; eyes as large as the crown of a hat; nose eight feet, eight inches long; a pair of shoulders 16 feet wide; legs 22 feet from hip to foot, filling a six-foot shoe; hands 32 by 52 inches and a grand total weight exceeding 100,000 pounds. As for the ox or turkey to be carved, we forbear to inflict so much weight and size as would be required upon our readers. . . . On the face of the blade, polished like a mirror, has been etched beginning at the shank (which is engraved and silver-plated) a likeness of William Penn, above and beneath it the words forming an arch, "Beaver Falls Cutlery Company." Separated from this by an ornamental line is the entire state coat of arms, shield surmounted by an American Eagle, Liberty, the shield itself, Protection. On the upper third of this is a ship at sea designating Commerce. Beneath it, a plow and sheaves of grain, implements of Agriculture. The horse rampant is supporting the shield, meaning strength and chivalry. The progress of husbandry, field of grain, shipping, etc., are seen in the distance. The third section near the point of the blade contains an accurate portrait of Governor Hartranft with his honest, manly face. The reverse centers on a simple etching of scrollwork and a mother sitting with her children at play.
>
> Of the fork, other than it is a companion of the knife, (weight total 130 pounds) little need be said. It has the patent spring-guard and the cost for grinding alone with the knife was $130.00. The steel for both was forged at Beaver Falls. The steel was trimmed and prepared by experienced workmen. The etching is a remarkable piece of work of its kind. The ivory carving on the handles is as perfect a piece of workmanship as can be found in the country. The above work was done by the regular employees of the Cutlery Company.

James Patterson Home. Located on the corner of Seventh Avenue and Third Street, it was also called the mansion house. This is where the Chinese workers who worked at the cutlery were housed.

According to another source, the prongs of the fork were 27 inches long and 6 inches wide at the base. On the spring guard are seen vines and clusters of grapes. It is said that the company also had at the exhibition a pocketknife containing 365 blades.

Edwin Clayton did the carving on the ivory handles of the giant pieces of cutlery. Mr. T.C. Moore did the etching on the knife blades.

The Cutlery Company exhibit at Philadelphia also contained a plaster-of-paris cast of the company trademark, depicting an American eagle flapping its wings in triumph over the British Lion. As the story goes, the trademark caught the eye of the British member of the awards committee. He was incensed at this and insisted that the committee bypass the Beaver Falls Cutlery exhibit; therefore, the exhibit was not considered for an award.

Whatever became of that gigantic knife and fork? Tableware of such proportion is difficult to hide and doesn't just disappear. The late Sidney Kane, who taught mathematics to generations of Beaver Falls students, decided to find out. He traced the pieces to the Cattaragus Cutlery in Little Valley, New York, which had obtained the set from the Beaver Falls Cutlery in 1887. In August of 1975, Kane hit the road in search of the showpieces. For awhile, the trail was hot. It zigzagged from Beaver Falls to Little Valley, and then to Springville, New York, then back to Little Valley. But there the trail cooled, and the best Kane could come up with was the intelligence that the knife and fork had been shipped from Little Valley to a destination in Wisconsin some time around 1970.

"In frustration, I returned to Beaver Falls," wrote Kane. So the mystery of who possesses the largest knife and fork in the world remains unsolved.

Another mystery is what became of the Chinese who worked at the cutlery. According to the *Beaver Countian*, "In 1877, the last of the Chinese left Beaver Falls. About half of them had left from time to time, but the remainder left as a group. The Cutlery Company as part of their agreement paid their fare back to San Francisco." However, many people think the Chinese families in the Beaver Falls and Pittsburgh areas are descended from this group, which suggests that some may have remained behind.

Some had died during their five years at the cutlery and they were buried in a cemetery in the vicinity of 28th Street and Fifth Avenue on College Hill. But the remains were removed, probably for return to China in keeping with tradition, and the cemetery no longer exists.

In *History of Beaver County Pennsylvania*, the Reverend Joseph H. Bausman tells us that in 1886, "the business having ceased to be profitable, the works were closed."

A number of concerns occupied the cutlery buildings after that business was discontinued. Among these were the Metric Metal Works, a producer of gas meters; The Eclipse Bicycle Company; The McCool Tube Company; the New York Pittsburgh Company, maker of typewriters and attachments for sewing machines for blind stitching; The Shelby Steel Tube Company; and The Beaver Falls Car Works.

For those fortunate enough to have pieces or sets of the ware produced by the Beaver Falls Cutlery, the firm may be gone, but it certainly is not forgotten.

Shortly before the turn of the century, Louis Ingram and Ernest Richardson (emigrating from England to the United States before 1900) were respectively general manager and plant superintendent of one of the pioneer producers of porcelain enamel signs in this country, Enameled Iron Company, then located at the foot of Steffin Hill in White Township.

They dreamed of establishing a company of their own and spent many nights in the basement of the old Book House in Beaver Falls, making plans for the venture. Their dream materialized in May of 1901, when the Ingram-Richardson Manufacturing Company was formed, its organizational meeting being held in the basement of Eckles Drug Store in the north end of Beaver Falls. Original incorporators joining Ingram and Richardson were Fred Davidson, Whitt Eckles, Ernest L. Hutchinson, Dr. James S. Louthan, and J. Rankin Martin. Operations were established in the buildings on the site of the former Midgely Belt Works on 24th Street Extension in Beaver Falls.

Soundly established on a modest scale by these two men, who were pioneers in the development of the porcelain enamel industry in the United States, Ing-Rich grew and was recognized as a leader within its industry. The factory at Beaver Falls was expanded from time to time to cover 120,000 square feet of productive floor space and at its peak operation, the company employed 600 people. Demand for tabletops from the kitchen cabinet manufacturers led the company to establish a plant in Frankfort, Indiana in 1915. This plant grew to the same size as the Beaver Falls operation. To encourage successful operation, the company arranged for the personnel at Frankfort to acquire management and ownership control, which was accomplished in the 1930s. The Frankfort operation became a separate company at that time.

From a technical standpoint, the company had a remarkable record for developing innovations in porcelain enameling in both processing and product. Ing-Rich was one of the earliest users of the acetylene welding technique when it pioneered a process for joining together flat sheets to produce a one-piece food compartment liner for ice boxes, the first of its kind in the United States. This is now used in all electric refrigerators.

In the early days, Ing-Rich was a pioneer user of continuous enameling furnaces and, in 1936, installed what at that time was the largest continuous electric enameling furnace in use. In sign production, Ing-Rich was the first company in the industry to successfully develop screen process methods for making signs, permitting the use of more intricate designs and providing substantial cost reduction from the old-fashioned brush and zinc stencil process.

The company was the first in this country to manufacture porcelain enameled steel tabletops, decorated top and leaf covers for breakfast dinette sets, porcelain enamel refrigerator linings, and gas heaters. Another Ing-Rich product was the first completely porcelain enameled gas kitchen range. Ing-Rich was the pioneer manufacturer of porcelain enamel license plates for automobiles.

During World War II, Ing-Rich converted to the production of vital war materials and in 1943, was recognized with the Army-Navy "E Award." At this time, the large enameling furnaces were used for heat-treating a wide variety of essential military products. Among the products Ing-Rich helped produce were armor plate, shell containers, and component parts for tanks and other vehicles and aircraft parts.

Following World War II, the company, facing declining markets in signs and tabletops because of public acceptance of plastics, entered the building construction market and became a major factor in architectural porcelain enameled panels for building exteriors, porcelain enamel steel chalkboards for schools classrooms, and porcelain enameled aluminum signs for the Federal Interstate Highway program.

Following the deaths of Louis Ingram and Ernest Richardson, in 1941 and 1949 respectively, the business was continued with the late J. Fred Ingram, son of Louis, as president. In 1965, ownership of the company changed hands by its acquisition through purchase by Park Electrochemical Company of New York and operations in Beaver Falls were soon discontinued.

Keystone Portable Steam Driller Company Limited was organized February 2, 1882 in the back room of James D. McAnlis's Jewelry Shop at the corner of Eighth and Main Streets with a stock of $20,000. On January 27, 1883, a board of

ING-RICH. This photo was taken during the 100th anniversary of the founding of the company. Pictured are Ernest Richardson's daughter Jean Merriman and sons Frederick, Richardson, and David.

five managers was elected, including the Reverend Dr. H.H. George, R.A. Patterson, R.M. Downie, J.D. McAnlis, and the Reverend R.J. George.

The manufacture of portable water well drilling machines was begun with an actual capital of $6,000 in a small stone building—the old Thornily Foundry and Machine Shop in Fallston. In 1887, the company purchased four building lots at 20th Street and Eighth Avenue (then Cedar Street), for $2,500. It erected two frame buildings and an office and moved into the new quarters late in the year.

Beaver Falls north of 12th Street was at that time a region of dirt roads, woods, and boulder-strewn fields. Improvements in design of the Keystone drill went hand in hand with the growth of the business. Numerous patents were taken out year after year by Downie.

The first machine was a non-traction single beam rig with a tri-pod derrick and was built by Downie and his brother in two sizes. The smaller machine had a 6-inch by 6-inch single steam engine and a 34-inch by 48-inch boiler and was recommended for a depth of 150 feet. Number 2 had a 6-inch by 8-inch engine and a 34-inch by 54-inch boiler and was good for wells of 300 feet in depth.

In 1887, after two years of experimentation, a traction attachment was perfected, which made the well driller independent of the convenience of customers' teams or teamsters, and effected a great saving in time and operating

153

expenses for a drill contractor. The company was rechartered as Keystone Driller Company in 1891.

The double-beam, two-sheave spudding device, "which has never been much improved upon" according to a 1926 book titled *The Story of Keystone Driller*, was developed and patented in 1892. The unique Keystone cross-tubular boiler was produced about the same time. "Its popularity was in favor as a prime mover for such machinery," the book stated.

About 1904, Keystone drills came into wide demand for bits, a patented vacuum sand pump, and adapted for placer gold testing in advance of gold dredging operations. Hundreds of machines were shipped to California, Alaska, Siberia, and other parts of the world for this purpose.

About 1904, Keystone drills came into wide demand for drilling large blast holes in cement and limestone quarries and heavy excavation jobs.

Probably the most outstanding advancement was the successful application in 1923, after many years of costly experimentation and engineering effort, of an approved four-cylinder gas engine to the motivation of the standard line of portable well drills.

In 1892, 41 machines were shipped from the plant, which meant about $75,000 to $100,000 worth of business. By 1899, sales reached a total of 94 drills and an annual total of about $250,000. By 1902, considerable expansion had taken place—several wooden buildings were added and about 100 men were employed at the plant. The company's great climb began in 1912. In July of that year,

KEYSTONE DRILLER. *Organized in 1882, the company left Beaver Falls in 1959. Keystone Driller employed 400 men and covered 9 acres. The site is now the campus of the Big Beaver Falls Area High School.*

Keystone Driller Company took the most significant step since its organization 30 years before—the company began to manufacture excavating machinery.

The output of "dirt loaders" in 1913 was three units. By 1917, the company was turning out 162 of the excavators in a year, including 14 new Model 6 15-ton all-steel outfits. In 1919, Keystone produced a four-roll skimmer bucket and hydraulic side jacks and a drop-bottom bucket was shown at the sales conference of January 1921.

A half-crawler was mounted under the rear end of the Model 4 machine in 1921 and 1922, but it was not successful. A half-crawler, or caterpillar traction, of outside manufacture was mounted under the front end of the machine in 1923, however, and was highly successful. Gas power was adopted in 1923 and 1924, and the first gas-driven machine was shipped in March 1924.

In 1926, the Beaver Falls plant covered about 9 acres and employed more than 400 men, most of then skilled mechanics. The plant stretched from 17th Street to 22nd Street and company property ran from as far east as Eighth Avenue (between 19th and 21st Streets) and west to the Pennsylvania Railroad tracks.

The company, which became Stardrill-Keystone in the 1950s and later a division of Koehring Company, left Beaver Falls in 1959, transferring all manufacturing operations to Springfield, Ohio.

For a brief period in history, Beaver Falls was making a bid to become the amusement ride center of the country. The effort came around 1920 from the Travers Engineering Company, which later became the R.E. Chambers Company, Inc., located along Walnut Bottom Run near Ing-Rich.

Travers Engineering made all types of amusement park rides, specially designed and constructed here. Counted among early achievements were the "Caterpillar," "The Whip," and the "Dodge 'em" cars.

The Depression of the 1930s caused the changeover to R.E. Chambers Company, Inc., but it continued to make park equipment. By this time, it was marketing the "Stratoship," "Laff in the Dark," "Rocket Cars," "The Duck," and the "Midget Auto Racer."

It was the auto racer that got the most attention. It had an automatic clutch, special small-sized industrial tires, and weighed about 900 pounds. A special track was built for it at the New York World's Fair in 1939. This was 60 feet by 200 feet, oval shaped with banked turns, and held 12 cars. Each car was operated solely by the driver, who could go as fast as 18 miles per hour. The auto racer was popular, but not a success since track construction had to be permanent.

R.E. Chambers later became a general machine shop. Some of the company's rides are still in service, including the popular "Turtle" at Kennywood Park in Pittsburgh, and the "Rocket Cars," "The Swing," and "The Caterpillar" at Conneaut Lake Park north of Beaver Falls.

One of the interesting sidelights of Beaver Falls history was the acquisition of a brickyard by H.J. Heinz and Thomas Noble in 1868. It was bought from a man named Interest four years after he started it. This brickyard was located between 15th and 16th Streets on Ninth Avenue at the site of the playground and old ballpark. Both Heinz and Noble were just out of college and ran it until 1872 when they sold it to John Endres, their foreman. Noble went out west and H.J. Heinz went to Sharpsburg and started his pickle business.

Ad Davidson Sr. sold coal to the brickyard.

Another of the late 1800 to early 1900 industries that spread the name of Beaver Falls beyond its boundaries was Knott Harker & Company. This was a foundry that produced mantels, grates, and all types of fireplace equipment. Founded in January 1884, it was located on 10th Avenue north of Eighth Street after a brief time in New Brighton. Officers of the company included Joseph Wilson, president; Joseph H. Knott, secretary and treasurer; and William G. Harker, superintendent. Capitalization was $50,000.

After Harker's death in 1907, Knott and Wilson, with Mrs. W.G. Harker, ran the company until 1912. When Mrs. Harker left the company, the officers in 1912 were F.K. Brierly, president; W.C. Peating, vice president; and J.W. Knott, secretary-treasurer. F.N. Beegle of Union Drawn purchased the company in July 1916 and the name was changed to Ideal Foundry. It became part of Republic Steel on October 6, 1932 when that firm purchased Union Drawn. The business was moved to Newton Falls, Ohio in 1939.

Also produced was casting for the draw benches of the cold draw machines for Union Drawn, which burned down around 1910.

With the closing of Babcock & Wilcox in 1987, Beaver Falls became part of the Rust Belt of towns and cities in the northeastern and midwestern United States with economies formerly based on the steel industry. Babcock and Wilcox (B&W) started out with 90 men in 1904 at the small plant of the Pittsburgh Seam-Less Tube Company in Beaver Falls. B&W was in the forefront of the production of boilers during World Wars I and II.

The first seamless chromium tubing in the United States was produced at this Beaver Falls plant. In 1928, B&W became the first commercial producer of stainless steel. In the 1960s, the plant produced over 600,000 tons of steel annually, making it one of the nation's 25 largest steel producers.

In August 1987, McDermott International Corporation announced it would close its B&W plants in Beaver County, Beaver Falls, Koppel, and Ambridge. With these closings, more than 1,500 workers lost their livelihood. B&W was laid to rest alongside J&L, Crucible, Armco, American Bridge, Hydril, and other companies in the steel graveyard that Beaver County became.

In 2002, Beaver Falls learned of the sale of Moltrup Steel Company and its possible closing, along with the possible closing of Republic Engineered Steels Company. The people of Beaver Falls will no doubt mourn the steel industry's passing for the many years of prosperity and security it brought them, but they will talk about its great past and then turn to the future.

As Beaver Falls enters the twenty-first century, the city has a new mayor, Karl Boak, who is working to revitalize its economy. A new educational complex is being built and the business district will be re-energized in 2003 with the opening of the new County Office Building at Seventh Avenue and 11th Street. This new facility will bring more than 300 workers back to downtown Beaver Falls.

The steel worker has become the computer operator and Beaver Falls has grown and changed with the times without losing its individual identity. The city is alive and well and will continue to prosper in the new century.

MAYOR OF BEAVER FALLS. Karl Boak is a native of Beaver Falls and a member of the Kiwanis Club, and was also Jaycees man of the year in 1995. Karl is married to the former Jean Sylvester.

BIBLIOGRAPHY

BOOKS AND ARTICLES

Bausman, Reverend Joseph H. *History of Beaver County Pennsylvania*. Beaver Falls: The Knickerbocker Press, 1904.

Bicentennial Committee. *Beaver Falls Edition 1776-1976*. Beaver Falls: Beaver County Publications, 1976.

Britten, Kenneth and Beaver Falls Historical Society. *Images of America, Beaver Falls*. Charleston, SC: Arcadia Publishing, 2000.

Centennial Corporation of Beaver Falls. *Historical Salute to the Centuries 1868-1968*. Beaver Falls: The Tribune Printing Co., 1968.

History of Beaver County, Pennsylvania. Philadelphia and Chicago: Warner, A. & Co., 1888.

Industrial World, The. Beaver Falls: Daily Tribune Special Edition, 1910.

Industrial Hive of the Great Keystone State. Beaver Valley: The Industrial Publishing Co., 1905.

Reader, F.S. *Old Brighton*. Beaver Falls: The Beaver Valley News, 1908.

NEWSPAPERS

"Fourth of July Souvenir." Beaver Falls: *Daily and Weekly Tribune*, 1892.

Beaver Falls Tribune, The Star, Beaver Valley News, Argus & Radical. 1881–1884.

Beaver Falls Weekly Tribune. September 8, 1897–July 5, 1906.

Daily News. May 18, 1899–1903.

Beaver Falls Review. 1921–1942.

INDEX